# Soulbroken

## A Guidebook for Your Journey
## Through Ambiguous Grief

## Stephanie Sarazin

balance

NEW YORK BOSTON

Balance
Hachette Book Group
1290 Avenue of the Americas,
New York, NY 10104
www.gcp-balance.com
https://twitter.com/gcpbalance

First Edition: October 2022

Balance is an imprint of Grand Central Publishing. The Balance name and logo are trademarks of Hachette Book Group, Inc.

The publisher is not responsible for websites (or their content) that are not owned by the publisher.

The Hachette Speakers Bureau provides a wide range of authors for speaking events. To find out more, go to www.hachettespeakersbureau.com or call (866) 376-6591.

Library of Congress Cataloging-in-Publication Data
Names: Sarazin, Stephanie, author.
Title: Soulbroken : a guidebook for your journey through ambiguous grief / Stephanie Sarazin.
Description: First edition. | New York, NY : Balance, 2022. | Includes bibliographical references and index.
Identifiers: LCCN 2022019460 | ISBN 9781538709757 (trade paperback) | ISBN 9781538709764 (ebook)
Subjects: LCSH: Grief. | Psychic trauma. | Life change events.
Classification: LCC BF575.G7 S275 2022 | DDC 155.9/37—dc23/eng/20220511
LC record available at https://lccn.loc.gov/2022019460

ISBNs: 978-1-5387-0975-7 (trade paperback); 978-1-5387-0976-4 (ebook)

Printed in the United States of America

LSC-C

Printing 1, 2022

*For my children, Sam, Ellie, and Abigail,*
*whose unambiguous love got me out of bed.*

*To the souls whose lights*
*have been dimmed by loss,*
*may something inside*
*serve as your match.*

"You will lose someone you can't live without, and your heart will be badly broken, and the bad news is that you never completely get over the loss of your beloved. But this is also the good news. They live forever in your broken heart that doesn't seal back up. And you come through. It's like having a broken leg that never heals perfectly—that still hurts when the weather gets cold, but you learn to dance with the limp."

—ANNE LAMOTT


"There is a life-force within your soul, seek that
    life.
There is a gem in the mountain of your body, seek
    that mine.
O traveler, if you are in search of That
Don't look outside
Look inside yourself,
and seek That."

—RUMI

This book reflects my personal experience, recollections, and insights. Some names and characteristics were changed, some events have been compressed, and some dialogue recreated. Any errors are my own.

# IN GRATITUDE

My parents, Ed and Phyllis Sarazin, and sister, Rachel, and brother-in-law, Brad Bowman.

My brother, Eric Sarazin, my life's greatest teacher without ever speaking a word.

My tri-family, Kerry and Jason McConnell, and Regen and Andy Newton.

My people: You know who you are and how much you mean to me. You are golden, girls.

My Chicago girls+: Katie Beacham, Sarah Klein, Stacy Bennett, and Scott Bennett.

My friends Carrie Bristol, Nadine Fairbrother, Joanne Grafinger, Kara Brown Lee, Beth Piqueras, Susan Lerch, Alice Bayer, Spring White, Molly Sly, Chrissy Dukiet, Joey Napierkowski, Jamie Valvano, Lilly Whorton, Beth and Joel Holliday, Kevin and Tina Caul, Mary Anne and Dave Johnson, Tara Charvat and Craig Thiebaud, Matt and Mercedes Vedock, Kim and Ben Hartmere, Brent Varnell and Drew Cline. Special thanks to Robin Whitfield and Bubba for all you've taught me about the equal treasures of friendship, love, and grief.

# In Gratitude

* * *

For helping my mind, body, and soul: Karen Velasquez, Dr. Sophia Caudle, Dr. Hope Seidel, Nancy Greenlee, Elizabeth Ogren, Leeann Heinbaugh, Gerry Powell and the team at Rythmia, and my friends from the Omega Institute Writer's Week. Oprah Winfrey for helping me wake up every Sunday. Amy Kline, a lantern of light who helped me to find my own.

For helping this book into the world: *Soulbroken* midwife and editor extraordinaire Nana K. Twumasi, as well as Kimberley Lew, Natalie Bautista, Alexandra Hernandez, and the rest of the talented team at Balance and Hachette Book Group.

My agent, Jim Levine; Courtney Paganelli, and the team at LGR Literary. Author and thought leader Denise Brosseau; my brilliant proposal editor, Genoveva Llosa; Adam Grant, for encouraging me to *Think Again*; Romi Neustadt, for reminding me to *Get Over Your Damn Self*; Julie Thompson, Bryan Wish, and the dedicated team at BW Missions.

My daily correspondent, lifeline, and dear friend, Peg Sullivan. Well played, God.

My manfriend, hiking partner, and first-reader Chris Jordan: Thank you for speaking my language; your spiritual partnership is among the greatest treasures in my life on the other side.

*　*　*

Taita Tito, who came to open my heart and did, and who remains there still.

Griff, whose love and loyalty over thirteen years have been an anchor.

My star, my daisy, and my arrow, who picked me up and hugged me tightly, who witnessed my grief more than anyone else and would ask "Are you okay?"

I am now.

This book is made possible by many, but none more than those who shared with me their stories of grief, hope, and healing. A deep bow of gratitude to you all, including Alison Coates, Eileen Flanigan, Jamie Livernois, Tameka Means, Beth Swanson and her beloved late mother, Judy Foley, Stephanie Pappanastassiou, and Stephanie Thornton, my soul sister and forever first phone call.

To those not listed, or whose names were changed: thank you for trusting me to share your story.

CONTENTS

# Then

It was an ordinary Tuesday morning when I opened my husband's laptop; mine wasn't working, and I was desperate to print something. Seconds after that mundane act, my world dropped out from underneath me. I discovered that my husband of eighteen years, the father of my three children, and the man I had adored for more than twenty years was not the loyal and crazy-in-love-with-me man I believed him to be. Had my morning work call not been canceled, or had I opened his laptop a minute later, I would have missed the "ping" of the email notification that appeared in the corner of the screen. The message confirmed my husband's renewed subscription to an online dating website. Opening that single email revealed countless others; some shocked me with the use of affectionate pet names and order confirmations for romantic gifts that I had not received. Others confused me with details that contradicted my reality; travel confirmations revealed secret trips, and time stamps verified that my own proximity hadn't impacted planning. One after the next, each message stunned me with new facts and forced me to confront a devastating new truth. It was like being hurled into an amusement park fun house; you know, the kind where each room disorients you—the floorboards shake violently, walls shrink and expand unexpectedly, and mirrors distort your image in unimaginable ways. The twisted, electronic version I had unwillingly discovered was far less "amusing" and not at all "fun." I desperately wanted out of the discombobulated reality that I had stumbled into, but click by click, the more I searched for an explanation, the more surreal the fun house became. The laptop of horrors continued to confess one horrific secret after another: he had been unfaithful for many years with many (many!) women. I was eviscerated by the sudden bend in reality; my marriage, my husband, my life weren't what I thought they were. My body tingled and panic spread to every cell, in a deep knowing that something was very wrong, that I was not safe.

I called him and told him to come home from work, then fell to the ground shaking, my morning breakfast soon in a pool of vomit on the floor beside me. I'm not sure how long I stayed there, numb, except for the electrical-like zaps in my head. My brain was short-circuiting with the memory of a terrifying amusement park ride I endured on my sixth birthday. The gravity-defying Rotor had spun faster and faster, and as I watched the floor drop away, I couldn't comprehend what was happening. I experienced a panic that I had never before felt and couldn't make it stop. Back then, I had also eventually fallen to the ground, weeping and immobile. But now, as an adult, my brain hustled to connect the dots of an impossible duality and organize what I saw with my eyes into a narrative that made sense in my head. Frantically digging for an answer in the filing cabinet of my mind, I struggled to connect a plausible story. But, like a reference librarian unable to locate an exact match, my brain offered me the next-closest thing instead—an excavated memory, as if to say, "I can't find a way to make sense out of what we're seeing right now, but I *did* find that you had a similar physiological response also activated by a surreal, reality-bending experience on the day you turned six." Both my mind and body were reacting in much the same way they had all those years before. Unable to comprehend in real time, my adult mind remembered the experience from childhood and summoned it forth, as a meager but better-than-nothing offer.

My old life was instantly gone, but I didn't know that immediately. It was not until the shock wore off and after a few sessions of couples' therapy that it became clear I was not married to the man I had promised my heart to nearly two decades before. He had become someone else, and somehow I never noticed. Or maybe this is who he had been all along, and I had just been unaware of that truth. We divorced shortly after. The trauma of making this discovery and the subsequent unraveling of my once-happy life left me in pieces. As I tried to make sense of losing my husband and the beautiful life we had built as a team, I came face to face with grief.

# Then

For the next three years, I was fortunate to have the steady guidance of Amy, my terrific therapist, whose help I sought out the day after my discovery. She patiently supported me through my grief, allowing me the opportunity to come to my own conclusions while also skillfully redirecting me when I spent too much time in the wrong direction. She had her work cut out for her, especially since I had no prior experience with therapy or with grief. I had gone through life peripherally aware of each, thinking that therapy was for people who didn't understand themselves and that grief was for those who had lost someone to death.

I couldn't have been more wrong about both, but soon learned I had been especially naïve about grief. I had expected that when it came, I would go through the five stages theorized by psychiatrist Elisabeth Kübler-Ross—denial, anger, bargaining, depression, and acceptance—in a neat, linear way and be done with it.[1] Instead, my grief turned out to be messy and so much more complicated. To my surprise, the stages came and went as they pleased, in no sequential order. At some point in the day, I would feel acceptance, only to have that peace ripped away by anger. The following day would look the same, or would unleash depression, then denial, and then shift back to anger. But perhaps more importantly, my grief would cycle through a stage the Kübler-Ross model didn't account for, the first sign my grief was different than that experienced when a loved one dies.

In time, I would learn that grieving the loss of a loved one who is still living—a partner to betrayal, a child to addiction, a parent to a degenerative disease—isn't the same as grieving the loss of a loved one to death. We don't hold a funeral or offer an affectionate eulogy in order to engage with our grief in a healthy way. Grieving the loss of someone still living is also not quite the same as the grief experienced by those coping with what therapist Pauline Boss first coined as ambiguous loss: when a loved one goes missing or their death can't be definitively confirmed (e.g., when a soldier dies in a war but the body is never recovered). Later, that definition was expanded to include a psychological absence with physical presence. For example, ambiguous loss occurs with Alzheimer's disease, traumatic brain injury, or other chronic mental health illnesses that can take away a loved one's mind or memory. It may also result from, as Boss defines it, "obsessions or preoccupations with losses that never make sense, e.g., suicides or infant deaths."[2] Yet this still wasn't quite a fit for me, since it is one thing to hope that someone presumed dead might not actually be and will return to us, and quite another to hope our loved ones who are definitely alive (sometimes living in the same house or a few miles away!) will return as they once were. For me, even Dr. Boss's impressive body of work didn't speak to my specific experience or describe the grief process I was seeking to define. While my loss wasn't ambiguous, my grief was, and without knowing how to navigate such grief, I started my long, experiential effort of trial and error.

My curiosity and desire to understand how to cope eventually led me to find myself along the way. But it wasn't done in the express lane, and it certainly didn't happen because I'm a highly evolved individual who found forgiveness and never thought of my old life again, amen. Not even close. First, I tried to find resources to navigate the kind of grief I was experiencing. While I came across plenty dealing with depression or divorce, I found a dearth of information on how to cope with my profound grief: the death of a husband who still lived and a marriage that I loved so dearly. In this quest, I discovered it wasn't that I was alone in my experience; others were going through their own reality-bending experiences, too. They just weren't talking about it. That's because the events that activate this grieving process are often internalized as shameful or embarrassing, so those suffering often minimize their loss, if not keep it private altogether, and isolate and grieve alone.

Without a guidebook to help me in my journey, I spent the first year trying to make sense of it on my own, as well as in my weekly sessions with Amy. After reading *Option B: Facing Adversity, Building Resilience, and Finding Joy* by Sheryl Sandberg and Adam Grant, I reached out to Adam, with whom I had briefly worked in the past. While some of the tools for healing—such as building resilience and journaling—described in the book helped, other tools the authors offered made it much clearer that my mourning was a close-but-not-quite cousin to Sandberg's, who had lost her beloved husband to an unexpected death. Adam encouraged me to continue examining and teasing out the differences. A few months later, with a more developed idea of ambiguous grief, I submitted my attendee application to the annual TEDWomen conference, which was, to my excitement, accepted.

In discussing the idea with other attendees, it became clear that the scope of ambiguous grief was bigger than I first imagined. Not only that, it was often initiated by circumstances that hadn't yet been in my awareness. The stories I heard were beyond heartbreaking: a bride left at the altar by a groom who changed his mind, a woman abandoned as a child by the mother whom she adored, a grandmother suddenly denied visitation with the grandchildren she treasured. Each spoke in hushed tones as they disclosed the truths surrounding a loss that they didn't know how to grieve. I started to wonder just how many others were eager to make sense of their ambiguous grief, too.

Inspired by the interest and feedback I received at the conference, I began sharing my struggles with grief online and was amazed by the responses I received. The circumstances about which my fellow grievers were grieving and why varied. For some, it was divorce or estrangement; for others, cognitive decline or mental illness. But the commonality was that they were all grieving the loss of a loved one still living, feeling alienated, and longing to understand. I found an interesting common denominator among myself and other ambiguous grievers and formed a hypothesis about exactly what might make this grief different. I shared it with others, including Dr. Sophia Caudle, a therapist I had seen for eye movement desensitization and reprocessing (EMDR) therapy—a horrible but ultimately amazing experience Amy recommended and which we'll explore later in this book. Since I was no longer her patient, Dr. Caudle and I decided to partner to investigate the process of this emotional state more deeply. Eventually, we produced and administered an assessment tool as well as a mixed-method exploratory survey, the results of which provided data that we used to co-author the Ambiguous Grief Process Model. Additionally, our research tried to quantify the number of ambiguous grievers in the United States, the results of which were remarkable. Considering conservative estimates of the number of people experiencing events that often trigger ambiguous grief (e.g., divorce, a partner's betrayal, death of a relationship, or a medical diagnosis like dementia or Alzheimer's), we estimated that 60 percent of the population was likely to experience ambiguous grief in their lifetime.

Since then, I have found that the nature of this grief may also create conditions for an intense emotional experience not everyone encounters. You've likely already experienced heartbreaking loss at some point in your life: a loved one who died, a beloved pet that ran away, a treasured friendship that dissolved, the dream job that let you go. All are understandably "painful experiences of overwhelming distress"; the very definition of heartbreak by the *Oxford English Dictionary*. If you think back through your own life, you can probably pinpoint the first time you felt heartbroken, because there is nothing else like it. Even now, in middle age, I still remember when heartbreak first hit me as a teenager.

But when we lose someone we love *and* we also lose a part of ourselves, it's something more. When *who* we have lost is so deeply connected to *who we are*, when we are inextricably linked not only to a *person* but to *our connection to them*, the loss of our relationship is often a loss of our own self. That is why such loss stretches beyond being heartbroken to being *soulbroken*. Though ambiguous grief may trigger this aching pain, it isn't a prerequisite to this plane of painful disconnection from self; the early loss of a parent/child relationship and widows grieving the death of their decades-long spouses describe this pain, too. It is a frightening and often destabilizing period of time, and since there is no physical death for ambiguous grievers, not only does our loss thrust us into unwanted change, we soon discover that our grief is not validated in the same way. Therefore, to be soulbroken is to be filled with anguish that is brought on by the loss of our love, our relationship, and ourselves, and, often, it is void of validation. If you know this pain, my deepest sympathies to you, not only for your loss, but for how you have been hurting.

I know this pain, too, which is why I was desperate and determined to find anything that would heal my wounds and lead me to recovery. Since then, my exploration into the depths of ambiguous grief has revealed many more truths— and not only about grief. But to find this, I had to open both my heart and my mind not only to understanding my own grief, but to learn how grief is met by others in different parts of the world. Everything was on the table, from traditional Western medicine involving therapy sessions with psychiatrists to Eastern medicine, alternative healing with herbs, and energy relief with acupuncture.

To that end, this book is a compilation of my ugly, beautiful, hard, and hopeful experience with the ambiguous grief process. Along with my own firsthand experiences, you'll read the gut-wrenching and heart-healing stories of other ambiguous grievers. You'll also learn about a myriad of modalities, including modern medicine, ancient meditation, and mystical healing ceremonies with sacred plants. Throughout each stage, you'll receive helpful tools and have the opportunity to explore your insights through guided exercises. You'll also examine the unassuming emotion that emerged as a common denominator in this process, and even though it may feel counterintuitive, I'll teach you how to use it on the path to recovery.

My intention in writing this book is to offer proactive insights to help those navigating ambiguous grief and suffering the painful loss of a loved one still living. While the stories and tools presented will resonate differently for everyone, if you are open, I suspect you will find, as I did, valuable learnings in each. However, I'm not a doctor, and this book is not intended to give medical advice. I urge you to talk honestly with your health care professionals about your grief and whether something in this book could be helpful in your quest for healing.

To get the most out of our time together, I encourage you to "pack" for the journey. You'll need an empty backpack held in your mind's eye (we'll fill it along the way), an open mind (or at least the willingness to be willing to new/different ideas), your intention, and a dedicated notebook to log your discoveries and work through the exercises. Take note of whatever comes up for you, even if it's a fragmented thought. Like any explorer on an expedition, you'll find that field notes along the way often prove invaluable clues later—so when in doubt, write it out! For me, this daily practice turned out to be a gift, reflecting an evolution of my fears and dreams, and empowering me with an unwavering determination that the heavy, unshakable sadness of my loss would not define me forever.

This is the manual I wish I had all those years ago, beginning with that painful, awful discovery and revelation that ripped the floor out from underneath me. I hope wherever you may be in your grief—be it from a painful discovery like mine, a divorce or end to a relationship, a life-changing medical diagnosis, a broken relationship with an addicted child, or something else—that by reading this book a flicker of hope is sparked in you, letting you know that despite society often not recognizing the depth of your loss, your grief is real, your

Then

struggle is valid, and healing is possible. If you are willing to put in the work, if you are eager and ready to find a way out of your grief—but don't know where to begin—this book is for you, and I am privileged to serve as your guide.

You've got this. Let's begin.

# MAP OF AMBIGUOUS GRIEF

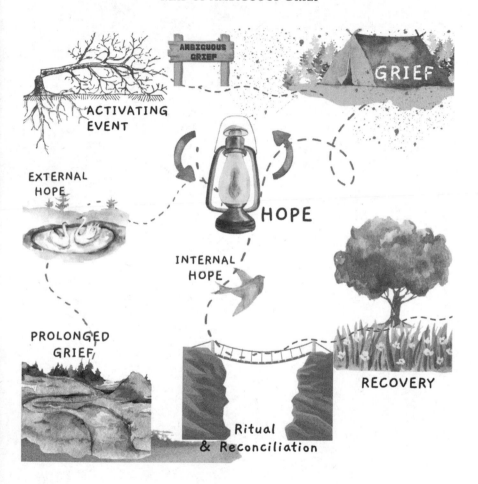

ACTIVATING EVENT

AMBIGUOUS GRIEF

GRIEF

EXTERNAL HOPE

HOPE

INTERNAL HOPE

PROLONGED GRIEF

Ritual & Reconciliation

RECOVERY

CHAPTER 1

# Activating Events, Estrangement, and Intention

"Begin as you mean to go and go on as you began."
—CHARLES H. SPURGEON, *ALL OF GRACE*

If you're suffering the loss of a loved one who is still living and you're in search of healing, I have some good news: feeling better is possible. I can understand where you're coming from—you didn't want to travel this road, and you didn't ask for this experience. Those of us suffering in this way tend not to be the ones who changed (or sometimes completely destroyed) the relationship. We may feel wronged, because it wasn't us who changed the dynamic of the relationship to begin with. Yet nonetheless, here we are, shattered and picking up the pieces. There are many reasons for experiencing this type of grief—it could be that you had to change the physical nature of your relationship (e.g., you filed for divorce, or you moved a loved one into a care facility)—but you likely did so in response to something. Throughout this book, this "something" is referred to as an **activating event**, the first component of the ambiguous grief process. Whatever it was, this event triggered your grief and has launched you into a new reality and led us to meet here.

You may not have chosen the circumstances that brought you here, any more than I chose mine or Dorothy Gale chose hers when she was swept up in a cyclone and dropped in Oz. You may feel like you've been dropped in Oz, too, and are alone and frightened as you seek to understand your new situation. While you can't undo the circumstances that have deposited you here in the Land of Ambiguous Grief, like Dorothy, you can take action to get to where you want to be. Perhaps that means finding your way back to your old life or charting a new life for yourself altogether. Maybe you are too disoriented or grief-stricken to think about your wants and needs right now, and that's fair, too. But whether you are seeking comfort, relief, understanding, or something else, you're likely reading this book because, at the very minimum, you're experiencing the emotional pain of a changed or lost relationship with someone you love. For some, these relationships may eventually resolve, and for others they may dissolve, but in either instance the emotional relationship as it once was is now gone, and you are no longer connected as you once were. This loss is compounded further by the fact that the person you are grieving is still alive; you may even still have contact with them. Just as this is a different kind of loss than one to death, so too is it a different kind of healing.

Understanding those differences will be key as you traverse the difficult days ahead.

## A PROCESS OF DISCOVERY

While the most trying days of my grief are now behind me, I remember them well. Largely because I processed the experience in real time and took mounds of notes. Whether talking to trusted friends or participating in individual and group therapy sessions, I became a keen observer, and I asked a lot of questions. Like a scientist on an expedition, I logged countless hours of observations. I interviewed authors and clinicians working in and around the grief space and studied other ambiguous grievers, too. In doing so, I uncovered patterns of behavior, and my own understanding grew. It became evident to me that the loss of an important love without a death may be just as painful, but that there are some important distinctions in how we struggle through our grief, namely the wrestling match with the emotion of hope, something grievers from death don't encounter. My hypothesis led to a research collaboration with one of my former therapists, and together we developed a survey that yielded hundreds of heartbreaking stories and important data insights that we used to co-author the Ambiguous Grief Process Model.[1]

Thanks to my own uncharted expedition through grief and the development of the Ambiguous Grief Process Model, I've sorted and organized those stacks of field notes into this guidebook. My intention is to provide you with a name for and understanding of the ambiguous grief process, as well as best practices for moving through it. I invite you to think of this book like a travel guide, with each component explored through a comprehensive travel-inspired framework. Every chapter will include the intimate stories of travelers who have visited here before you, complete with some facts on the activating event that brought them here. Like any good guide, I will also highlight my best tips and tools for you to consider at each stop. I also provide a collection of resources at the back of the book, including a quick-reference summary of helpful re-routing tools.

## THE AMBIGUOUS GRIEF PROCESS

As we embark on our journey, let's get acquainted with our map: the Ambiguous Grief Process Model. Made up of four main components, the ambiguous grief process is ignited by an activating event—the event that triggers a loss. Next begins the messy dance with the uncoordinated feeling state of grief, followed by the presentation of hope and an ensuing battle between her two personalities (see the chart below), the winner thus determining one of two options: a course set toward an all-consuming grief or a path that leads to your well-earned recovery.

In model form, it looks like Figure 1.1.

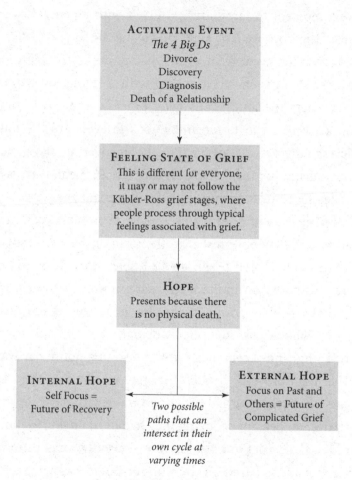

Source: ©CAUDLE and SARAZIN, 2018

Fig 1.1

Chapter by chapter, we will trek through each component of the Ambiguous Grief Process Model in depth. So, just as you would review a travel itinerary in advance of a big trip, take a moment to familiarize yourself with a general overview of the stops we'll be exploring along the way.

**Activating event**—An event that prompts troublesome feelings, changes the relationship with a living loved one, and triggers the ambiguous grief process. The most common activating events for ambiguous grievers are the four "Big D's": divorce, discovery (i.e., the uncovering of a major secret), diagnosis (e.g., dementia, addiction, mental illness), and death of a relationship (e.g., familial estrangement).

**Feeling state of grief**—A personal and unique experience that may or may not present in the form of the well-known grief model authored by Elisabeth Kübler-Ross. Though her work was based on individuals facing imminent death, we found the people in our study also experienced the grief stages Kübler-Ross identified—denial, anger, depression, bargaining, and acceptance—and did so in a nonlinear way. Rather than proceed through the steps one by one, they felt each stage both in varied order and unpredictable intensity, with over 60 percent believing they had been unable to move through their grief in a healthy way. Recently, an additional stage was added based on the work of David Kessler, a grief expert and co-author with Kübler-Ross. That stage is *meaning*, and it's one we'll reflect on as well.

**Hope**—A majority of the participants in our study experienced an additional stage in their grief, one not found in other models: the feeling of hope. Further, we found that an ambiguous griever cycles in and out of two distinctly different kinds of hope: external hope—hope that their loved one will return as they once were—and internal hope, which is focused on the self, on creating a better "new normal." How ambiguous grievers navigate this stage is an important factor in determining whether the griever is bound for recovery or a life consumed by their loss.

**Complicated grief**—This is a diagnosable mental health condition showing the occurrence of a persistent and pervasive grief response characterized by the longing for or preoccupation with the deceased, accompanied by intense emotional pain. The term complicated grief was updated to the term "prolonged grief disorder" in the fifth edition of the *Diagnostic and Statistical Manual of Mental Disorders*, published in 2020. Along with the presentation of intense emotional pain, prolonged grief disorder is diagnosable with three of the following symptoms: disbelief, identity confusion, avoidance of reminders of loss, numbness, loneliness, meaninglessness, and difficulty engaging in ongoing life.

**Recovery**—Ambiguous grievers can manage their grief and return to a state of being no longer centered on their loss. By practicing daily self-focus, being present- and future-oriented, and no longer directing energy to their lost relationship, the griever creates a space to move forward with their life. They do so with a healthy understanding of their grief but are not defined by it.

---

### Exercise 1 | Check-In

Having reviewed our "itinerary," take a moment to reflect by responding to these prompts in your journal.

Now knowing what is ahead on the itinerary, I am feeling:

Behind that feeling, the thought I am having is:

The stop I am most looking forward to exploring and why:

The stop I am least looking forward to exploring and why:

---

## PREPARING FOR OUR JOURNEY

Before we begin to understand why our experience feels different than loss from a physical death, it's important to get clear on a couple of key points: who we are grieving and what propelled us here. Depending on your relationship and your loss, sorting through your grief may be more difficult than any loss you've experienced before. Just as Newton's third law of motion recognizes that every action in nature creates an equal and opposite reaction, so, too, love creates an equal and opposite reaction: grief. Or, said another way, the depth of our grief is equal and opposite to the depth of our love. We can test this by thinking of the love we have (if we have any) for our mail carrier or coffee shop barista; it is not as strong as the love we have for our parent or partner or child. The intensity of feelings we experience when our mail carrier transfers or our barista quits is substantially less painful than the grief we experience when, for example, our parent's cognitive decline causes them not to remember us or our partner becomes addicted to drugs.

So, to be in deep grief is to have loved deeply. Be proud of that. You wasted nothing by deeply loving another person, and grief is a normal, expected, and healthy response to your loss. The father of modern psychology himself, Sigmund Freud, presented this idea over one hundred years ago, identifying mourning as a painful, albeit normal process.[2] In order to understand that, I had to experience grief firsthand and let go of an idea that I needed "fixing." Doing so allowed me to recognize that grief is not a condition to cure; rather, it is a human condition to be honored. Depending on your life experience, you may have already been through the ambiguous grief process more than once. Your loss(es) and subsequent grief may have occurred decades ago or perhaps just this week, but if grief is the price we pay for love, then in order to grieve, we need to take an honest inventory of who and what we have lost. It may take courage to be honest about this, but it's important that you are.

---

*Exercise 2 | The Focus of Your Grief*

For the purpose of our focus on ambiguous grief, first circle the relationships you have lost from causes not due to death. Next, if you have grieved or are grieving more than one, add a star next to the relationship loss that prompted you to pick up this book. Reflect on this specific loss as we encounter exercises throughout the journey. You can return to the exercises with another relationship in mind, but be sure to keep your focus on one person at a time.

| | | |
|---|---|---|
| Aunt | Fiancée | Significant other |
| Brother | Grandparent | Grandchild |
| Cousin | In-law | Uncle |
| Daughter | Mother | Nephew |
| Father | Sister | Niece |
| Friend | Son | Partner/spouse |

Is your specific relationship listed? If not, add it to the list. Keep this relationship in mind as we work through the process.

---

## WHAT BROUGHT YOU HERE?

Just as you are thinking about this book as a guide through your grief, think of an activating event as the vehicle that brought you to this place. Whether that event launched you like a rocket or delivered you with the gentleness of a soft breeze, your passport has been stamped! No matter how you arrived, let's honor your loss by identifying your activating event. This is an important step because we can't heal from that which we can't acknowledge. If we want to feel better and be willing to learn how to grieve our loss in a healthy way, we have to come to terms with the truth, no matter how painful. Working with half-truths or truth by omission won't serve us here, even though it may be tempting! For me, minimizing what happened may have been less painful ("I discovered an affair") or burying my discovery like it didn't happen ("what affair!?") may have avoided pain altogether, but a false narrative in any form is an obstruction to true healing work. It can also create what psychologists call cognitive dissonance, a state of anxiety that is caused by simultaneously holding two contradictory truths. We have enough to sort through already, so let's be honest about this from the start. Doing so is the best way to begin and will safeguard you from the energy-sucking excursion to cognitive dissonance.

## ID Your AE

As we briefly covered in our itinerary overview, the trigger that takes us from love to grief and begins the ambiguous grief process is an activating event. This is the experience of learning new information that impacts a relationship with a loved one who is still living, thereby changing or ending the relationship as it once was. This may be a singular, traumatic event (e.g., a discovery like mine or an event like Dorothy's, a brain injury sustained during a cyclone). It could also be a series of moments that build over time and culminate with an event you've been dreading, such as your loved one's formal diagnosis of Alzheimer's or the indoctrination of your beloved into a cult or gang. Whether your grief was triggered by an event you feared was coming or that took you by complete surprise, it has likely changed your life in significant ways. Some activating events are listed below. In thinking of the person you're grieving, pause to identify your activating event. Remember, these are significant life events involving a person you love deeply.

---

### Exercise 3 | Identify Your Activating Event

Thinking of the person you identified earlier, circle the activating event that caused the change in your relationship. It's common for more than one to apply.

Accident
Addiction
Alzheimer's disease
Brain injury
Broken engagement
Cognitive decline
Diagnosis
Disclosure of a secret
Discovery of a secret
Divorce
Familial estrangement

Gender identity
   change
Incarceration
Indoctrination (cult,
   gang, religion, etc.)
Job loss
Mental health crisis
Rejection
Retirement
Self-identity change
   (e.g., empty nester)

Is your activating event listed? If not, add it now.

If you are able, take a moment to honor yourself with a kind word and a cool drink of water before continuing. You've just completed a difficult task in acknowledging who you've lost and how it happened. Though you did not endure the distressing experience of the physical death of a loved one, you can equip yourself with tools that may help to aid or ease the ache.

---

*Exercise 4 | Your Honest Statement*

In your journal, combine the who and the how of your grief into one truthful statement:

I am grieving the loss of my _____ due to

_____.

---

# GRIEVING THE DEAD AND GRIEVING THE LIVING: WHAT'S THE DIFFERENCE?

If we live long enough, it is likely we can and will identify numerous times when we have experienced the loss of a loved one both with and without a physical death. In both cases, grieving can be exacerbated if the loss is unexpected or traumatic. What's also true for both is that how and why the relationship ends can impact the way we respond and go on living. A fundamental difference between the two, however, is that physical death itself isn't a new concept to us. Our species has evolved to understand that death is a part of life, and over time has established some things to "do" when physical death occurs. However, for loss that isn't caused by a physical death, we aren't as far along in how we cope—largely because this kind of loss is often barely acknowledged, much less processed, so there isn't much we "do." I'm not suggesting losing a loved one to death is an easy experience—far from it—but it's important we distinguish that grieving the loss of a loved one because they have died is different than grieving a loved one who is still alive. If you've experienced both, you'll recognize this subtle distinction; the ambiguous grief process is indeed a different kind of loss and a different kind of healing. Let's take a closer look at how we deal with each of them.

## Grief via Physical Death

I'm not the first to tell you that we aren't immortal—we will eventually pass on from this life, as have the billions of souls who lived before us. And while, as a society, we aren't great at doing grief, we are aware that grief is a part of death. With that, humans have established some generally agreed-upon ways in which we cope with loss by death, such as family and friends at funerals, heartfelt homilies, effusive eulogies, and freezers filled with frozen foods. We bury bodies or spread ashes as a finality to physical death, and often that is the extent of our generally accepted customs of coping. Even if death was a welcome reprieve for the departed, this entire experience can be exhausting and highly emotional for loved ones.

For those mourning or merely in the orbit of the bereaved, death and grief can be uncomfortable. In our discomfort, we've become unwitting performers, delicately tiptoeing around the grief-stricken, careful not to make reference to the dearly departed—or, worse, say their name! (Gasp!) Or should we? (Sigh.) We don't know! (Ugh.) So we often fumble through conversations like bad actors who haven't studied their script. Without knowing what we're supposed to say, we use someone else's words instead and send a store-bought sympathy card as our ambassador. Sometimes, we are so uncertain of what to say or do that we do nothing at all, or maybe we do the accepted minimum, and "heart" a post. We walk a tightrope of trying to balance what to do and say with what not to do and say. Maybe we attend the wake, send flowers, or donate to a special charity. We want to be supportive, yet it's uncomfortable because we don't want the experience or feelings for ourselves, as if grief were contagious. As a result, some of us just avoid the Grief Cooties altogether, vaccinating ourselves with excuses or staying away from the afflicted in hopes of preventing the spread.

These interactions show us that we are often lousy performers when it comes to grief—and we may not even realize it. Not because we are terrible people, but because we don't know what to do or say, because navigating grief in a healthy way likely wasn't taught to us or modeled in our homes and communities. And remember, this is the inevitable loss and subsequent grief of death—an inescapable human condition!

So, if as a whole, we're lousy at "doing" grief due to physical death, how do you think we handle grief when it is birthed from a more ambiguous space, like an activating event? Do we even have sympathy cards for that?

## *Grief via Activating Event*

---

**Ambiguous:** lacking clarity or definitiveness; obscure, indistinct. Of doubtful or uncertain nature; difficult to comprehend, distinguish or classify. (*Webster's Dictionary*)

**Ambiguous grief:** the feeling experienced from the loss of a loved one who is still living, accompanied by a change in or death of the relationship.

---

In 2017, when I was first trying to understand why my grief felt different, I came upon the term "ambiguous loss," first coined in 1999 by Pauline Boss. This was based on her work with individuals whose loved one's death was itself ambiguous—meaning that, due to circumstances surrounding the loss, death was not confirmed (e.g., a solider missing in action, a kidnapping, a natural disaster, etc.). Such an unknown often creates a grief-like purgatory in which loved ones wait for word in an ongoing vigil, hoping tomorrow will bring proof of life and the return of their loved one. In my case, there was definitely no physical death—but I recognized that while my loss was not ambiguous, my grief was. Finding nothing specific to my grief and inspired by Dr. Boss's observation of ambiguous loss, I started to pay close attention to my grief and what, if anything, was missing from my mourning. If I could just find whatever that was, I felt certain I could find a way out of my pain. In the coming chapters, we'll dig into the host of reasons that proved more difficult than I had anticipated, largely due to what I consider to be a disfunctional grief culture.

We have established that, in our modern world, we soothe the pain of grief from death with events like funerals, while with ambiguous loss, we continue to wait, lighting candles in vigil in an effort to assuage our grief. But what do we do when there is no physical death or chance of reunion? Unlike these heartbreaking losses, the ambiguous grief experience may be even more, well, ambiguous. As such, it doesn't tend to yield the same kind of support. I wasn't a widow, and the love from my marriage hadn't been preserved as it would have been had my husband died a physical death on that terrible Tuesday morning. Instead, my relationship died by way of an activating event, my marital death certificate citing "death by discovery" as the cause.

How then does this alter or influence our common grieving practices? There were no public eulogies from old friends, no cousins bestowed the honor of pallbearer. I wasn't afforded the gift of donning black and receiving a line of hugs and condolences from those who knew and loved my husband, too. I didn't keep his memory alive by starting a scholarship fund in his name or by regaling our children with countless stories of his antics or our many years together. Instead, I was unsure what to tell my children or anyone else. Not only were there no commonly prescribed societal practices—like a funeral—to initiate during this time, but I quickly realized that in my situation (and in that of some other activating events), nefarious feelings of shame and embarrassment often emerge along with the sometimes-devastating details of the loss. In my case, aside from disclosing the full truth to Amy, and one trusted friend, I said nothing to anyone else and went radio silent, citing contrived illnesses or overbooked schedules to hide my plunge into isolation.

Thankfully, that friend, who is also named Stephanie, met me with compassion and empathy every day for eight weeks, which was instrumental in helping me eventually emerge from embarrassed isolation. She spurred the truth within me, which was that I had honored my marriage and any eruptions of shame or embarrassment were not mine to carry. The truth was that I was devastated and seeking to find my way through the pain, and if others wanted to cast judgment, it was not my concern. Two months after my activating event, I picked up the phone and finally broke the difficult news to my family and friends. These nuances and how you navigate them will ultimately be up to you, but for me, accepting that my loss and subsequent grief were different than loss via death propelled me to question many things. First among them, my own behavior: had my husband died, I surely wouldn't have waited two months to send word to my family and friends!

Fast-forward several months, and I grew compelled to uncover why this grief felt different. That answer began to emerge a year later as I dove into survey results and began interviewing others. Excavating through those responses, and later through details from interviews, two treasures emerged. I wish I'd had these during the immediate aftermath of my activating event, but I'm so delighted to share these two gems with you now. I hope this good word reaches you sooner rather than later, dear traveler:

1. There is a name for what you are experiencing.
2. You are not alone in your anguish.

## WHAT WE CARRY

Moving through the wide range of difficult emotions and psychological processing experienced after an activating event isn't a journey many travelers reflect upon with fondness. For some, the event has induced trauma, and specific support from trained professionals may be necessary to cope (more on that in Chapter 3). For others, it may not have been traumatic, but was nonetheless painful and confusing. In either instance, now that you've named the activating event that has brought you here and examined the differences that make your grief unique, you have one more exercise left to complete before moving on: you will be well served to create your own version of Dorothy's ruby slippers—a powerful talisman to fortify you against whatever obstacles await you on the path ahead. It must be easily accessible, available to you whenever needed, and in your full and careful protection. Though you will carry it deep within your heart, instead of on your feet, it will guide you just the same: it is the creation and practice of your intention.

## Intention

The concept of intention isn't some mystical-speak born out of counterculture. Philosophers and spiritual leaders alike have been sharing its importance for millennia; it is referenced in religious texts and cited in lectures stretching to antiquity. In Hebrew, the word *kavanah* defines intention as the sincere direction of the heart. Intention can also be thought of as a specific act of mentally determining a desired action or result—it is the definitive purpose or attitude that sets our actions in motion. So, in deciding how you want to act through this process (or any circumstance in life), you must first become clear on how you *intend* to act. Intention is more than merely thinking a thought. It's purposefully developing the thought, declaring the thought, and then committing to the thought through our actions. I know, I know—easier said than done, but it is doable, and ultimately, setting and committing to your intention is a wildly empowering act. If there is great power in purposefully declaring and practicing your intention, think conversely about what it is like to live without intention. In making this choice, we render ourselves susceptible to the thoughts, actions, and intentions of others. (No thanks!)

Even before I knew I was on a quest to heal, the very first piece of gear I acquired was my intention. I set an intention to stay in my integrity and practice compassion for myself and my family as I navigated my divorce. To call upon love and not anger and to remain steadfast in who I truly was. Ironically, I discovered its power quite unintentionally while attempting to cope with my activating event. My intention was born from my higher self, or what I call "the Me of My Soul." At all hours, it whispered comforts and affirmed me with words I didn't know I had, my favorite being: "I know who I am." The "Me of the World," or the me that is packaged and perceived by how I appear or what I own and have accomplished, was well justified in being angry for what I'd discovered and how my world had been upended. I certainly didn't want to spiral, nor did I want to become cynical or vengeful. Simply tune in to any video streaming service for innumerable plotlines depicting a woman scorned who descends into her worst self, leaving wreckage strewn in her wake. That wasn't who I was when I entered my marriage, and that wasn't who I wanted to be as it ended. My "soul self" gifted me my intention and fortified my resolve that the painful betrayal wouldn't take the best parts of me or change me for the worse. This isn't to say I nailed it. Sometimes, I didn't show up as my best self—I said things out of anger, spiraled into skeptical thoughts, and wallowed in worry. But, thanks to my intention, that behavior was the exception, not the norm.

Depending on your relationship and your activating event, your intention may be more specific or more general than my own. For example, for the grieving wife with a partner experiencing cognitive decline, her intention might be to practice patience no matter how frustrating the circumstance. For an adult daughter estranged from her father, her actions may evolve from one of two different intentions. In one scenario, she may set an intention to teach her father a lesson, and in another she may set an intention to establish firm boundaries with him. Notice the difference in how each intention feels. While the former is punitive, with an "I'll show him," vengeful attitude, the latter is rooted in ownership and has an "I'll do this for me," self-care attitude. In either case, she commits to do so by ignoring his attempts for contact and returning his gifts. While the actions may appear the same to the father, the intention—whichever one she sets—will ultimately yield consequences aligned with that intention for the daughter.

Whether these examples resonate with you or not isn't important. Your intention is as personal as the loss you are grieving, and regardless of your current situation, the tool of intention is available to you. My intention became my compass, guiding my direction through a foreign land. As with any overly confident traveler, it was always clear when I tried to navigate without it: I inevitably ended up lost, frustrated, and doubling back to course-correct and find my way once more.

## Exercise 5 | Setting Intentions

As you contemplate your intention, return to your journal to complete the following prompts:

As I grieve the loss of my _____,

I feel _____, _____, and

_____. It doesn't feel good when I am acting

_____ and _____.

I feel at my best self when my behavior is

_____ and _____.

When you have clarity, write your intention in a complete sentence:

My intention as I navigate this difficult season of the ambiguous grief is _____

A mantra to remember this may also be helpful. For me, my intention was summed up with the phrase, "I know who I am." Reciting those words encapsulated my intention, which I called upon often. I even made it into a piece of art hanging on my wall so I can see it daily. What might be a mantra that expresses your intention? If you aren't sure how to phrase yours, reread your intention and add the word "because" to the end of it, then see what comes up for you as you finish that sentence.

For example: My intention is to stay in my integrity and be compassionate toward myself and others, to call upon love, not anger, and to stay steadfast to my true self...because...that is who I am, and *I know who I am.*

---

Notice that intentions can be set from a place of love, as with the loved one with Alzheimer's, or fear, as with the estranged daughter. An intention that is focused on you and what you can control (yourself) is key; an intention that is contingent on the actions of another person will serve you as well as a broken compass. As you think about setting your intention, be sure to cross-check yourself by asking, "Is this an intention rooted in love, or something else?" Keep reworking it until your answer is love.

## THE ESTRANGED FATHER

John, the father of the estranged daughter referenced earlier, may never fully know why his daughter returned his gifts or the intention of her actions, but, as he shared with me, it was clear that he understood a powerful concept: a relationship requires two people who want to be in shared experience with one another. As much as he may desire a healthy father-daughter relationship, his actions, thoughts, feelings, and intentions cannot force that into being. I spoke to John about the estrangement with his daughter, which took him by surprise when, shortly after her nineteenth birthday, he came home from work to find the birthday packages he had mailed to her a week earlier. He was further confused to recognize "RETURN TO SENDER" written in his daughter's handwriting. His calls and texts went unanswered as he tried to understand what had gone wrong.

"By the next day, I was beginning to get worried," he said. "I live a four-hour drive away, but decided I needed to go check on her in person. In preparing to leave, it occurred to me to open the package, and that's when I found her letter inside. Her letter went on and on, listing how I'd let her down after her mom and I divorced and how I should have done better since she's the only daughter I have. She said it many different ways: she was ending our relationship and wanted nothing to do with me."

John told me, "Of course, I've made mistakes as a father, though I can't see how I deserve a punishment this extreme, you know? I was especially blindsided since we had spent a fantastic two weeks together just a month before! So, what could I do in that situation? She's an adult, so I can't force her to visit with me, to talk to me, to love me."

It had been five years since the onset of estrangement with his daughter, yet his grief was visible as we spoke. He shared that in the first year, he made further attempts to connect with her, calling more and sending emails as well as cards and gifts. Anything sent via snail mail was returned unopened. "I checked each one hoping to find a letter from her inside. At that point, even an angry letter would have been better than the silence."

Overwhelmed and embarrassed, John didn't disclose his grief to friends and minimized the estrangement when her name came up with family members. Eventually, he sought support from a therapist, who helped to empower him with what he could control. "With the help of my therapist, I started to understand that my own actions toward her were causing me more suffering and maybe even unintentionally making things worse between us. I spent a lot of time trying to make things right between my daughter and me, and it took a toll on my whole life, my job, my marriage, my friendships. I can't imagine not feeling a level of sadness as long as we are estranged," he said, "but I'm now at a place where I understand that no relationship can be forced—even those that we presume are forever because they are our own blood. Eventually, I had to turn my energy back to myself and give myself an opportunity to heal—maybe even thrive—without her."

John's story illustrates a point worthy of attention: it isn't that he no longer experiences sadness or that he never thinks of his daughter because his grief is "cured," but rather that he has found a way to live with his grief by redirecting energy to himself and not to her. When he is tempted to expend that valuable force on a relationship that does not exist, he remembers what he learned while working with his therapist: "In my final email," he shared, "I let her know that I love her and will welcome her with open arms when and if she wants to see me again. Until then, I will honor her wishes and not contact her. It was so hard to say that, and then, later, even harder to actually do it. I didn't want her to feel like I'd given up, because that isn't why I stopped reaching out. She recently graduated with her college degree, and I felt such a heightened void that whole week, so I specifically planned some time to be good to myself and focus on the love I do have around me. It's surreal that my little girl had such an important milestone in her life, and I wasn't there for it. I don't know what other milestones are coming and if I'll be part of those, so I try not to worry about that. Whether or not she chooses to see me again, it doesn't change the fact that I love her and pray for her daily— and that she will live in my heart always."

John set an intention to love her from afar, without additional pleas for conversation, and chose to spend that energy compassionately loving himself as he lives without her.

---

*Exercise 6 | Huddle Up*

Before we move on to the next stop, let's make sure we've fully embraced our first. Grab your journal and complete the following sentences:

I am grieving the loss of: _____

My activating event was: _____

My mantra is: _____

My intention is: _____

Tuck these into your imaginary backpack. We will be using them frequently as we trek on, starting with our second stop: the shit-show shantytown known as the Feeling State of Grief.

---

Keep in mind, there is no time limit to how long you stay at each "stop," so go at your own pace, pause when you need to reflect, process, or rest, and then continue on—with intention—when you're ready.

## WISE WORDS ON INTENTION

"Every action, thought, and feeling is motivated by an intention, and that intention is a cause that exists as one with an effect. If we participate in the cause, it is not possible for us not to participate in the effect."

—GARY ZUKAV

"When our intentions toward others are good, we find that any feelings of anxiety or insecurity we may have are greatly reduced. We experience a liberation from our habitual preoccupation with self and paradoxically, this gives rise to strong feelings of confidence."

—HIS HOLINESS THE 14TH DALAI LAMA

"It [intention] is the principle by which I rule my company and the principle by which I rule every action in my life."

—OPRAH WINFREY

"Actions are according to intentions; everyone will get according to what they intended."

—THE PROPHET MUHAMMAD

CHAPTER 2

# The Feeling State of Grief, Cognitive Decline, and Minding Your Mind

"Caregiving often calls us to lean into love we didn't know possible."
—TIA WALKER

"We lost her too early. And we lost her while she was still on this earth. That seems particularly confusing at times."
—BETH SWANSON

I made her bed with the new clean sheets and comforter, and then added the green accent pillow for a pop of color. I placed the toothbrush holder, laundry basket, and wastebasket in the bathroom. I arranged pictures of family and friends throughout the room—on shelving and walls— loving all the memories those pictures held and hoping they would help her hold on to those memories as well. Everything looked perfect. We were ready for the next chapter in her life's journey. I always imagined living out this scene with my daughter as I helped her move into her first college dorm. Feelings of joy, anxiety, sadness, and pride would swirl throughout our activities as we set up the room, but ultimately, we would celebrate her next chapter. I would be thrilled for her life ahead.

But I wasn't moving my daughter to college just yet; she was only just starting high school. The room I was preparing was for my mother. After a ten-year battle with Alzheimer's, her care needs had grown beyond what a loving husband and family could provide. At 77, my mom would be moving into her new room at a memory care facility in my neighborhood. Setting up that room allowed me time for reflection and clarified a number of thoughts and feelings, underscoring the ache that life seemed unfairly out of order.

—ENTRY IN BETH'S JOURNAL, JULY 31, 2018

## THE ACTIVATING EVENT OF COGNITIVE DECLINE

Traumatic brain injury, dementia, Alzheimer's, and other types of cognitive decline are activating events that can trigger the ambiguous grief process. For Beth Swanson and for others loving aging family members through cognitive decline, the intimate nature of the process can make life uniquely difficult. Unlike the activating event stories highlighted thus far, wherein the nature of divorce and familial estrangement means that the ambiguous griever has little to no interaction with the loved one they are grieving. By contrast, those griev-ing the loss of a living loved one due to a degenerative brain disease or cognitive decline are often the very ones drafted as front-line caregivers. This involvement ensures frequent, often daily, contact and thus many moments of heartache. As loved ones change before us, the relationship changes as well. Whether an adult child assumes the new role of parent-ing their parent, or a spouse pivots to support the childlike needs of their partner, such transitions force a new relation-ship dynamic that can be difficult to accept. Understandably, the familial caregivers taking on these positions often face conflicting and even confusing feelings; for example, experi-encing both love and resentment, or feeling guilt along with a strong sense of duty.

Like many in her position, Beth was juggling a busy career and raising a family, which left little time for her own self-care and processing a wide range of new feelings. Reflecting on the previous ten years since her mother's diagnosis of Alz-heimer's disease, she writes:

"I acknowledged that my mother was never able to be a true resource for me as I raised my children. She couldn't answer many questions I wished that I could ask her—like 'how high can a fever be before I need to worry?'—because, as the disease progressed, she would only seem to remember and focus on negative information. I swiftly learned to report that 'all was great' with the kids, work, and family. That kept her spirits up and the conversation happy, but it was not the relationship I had expected or hoped for. My mother was also my friend, and I desperately wanted my children to know her as I did. But as the disease quickly progressed, it became clear that they wouldn't.

"It was frustrating for my father, too. He wished he could tell friends something more relatable, like 'she is recovering from surgery,' so then people would pitch in, bring meals, and ask how treatment was going. And we both desperately want to be able to describe a potential light at the end of tunnel—a cure on the horizon or even a promising medication—but there is no light with Alzheimer's. As of now, very few medications even slow the disease.

"On top of it all, Alzheimer's is isolating, not only for the patient, but also for the spouse, caregivers, and family members. Very few people seem to know how to react, respond, or offer support. My father and I were totally unprepared for the amount of time we would need to devote to managing this disease."

## CAREGIVER GRIEF

For Beth and the caregivers of some 6 million people living with Alzheimer's in the United States, urgent support is needed. In learning from Beth and others in this position, it's no wonder that those grieving the loss of a living loved one due to cognitive decline may need additional support relative to other ambiguous grievers. This complex relationship dynamic, coupled with sustained focus on the needs of their loved one and not themselves, results in the griever/ caregiver's self-care needs often going unmet. A 2019 study published by the Alzheimer's Association revealed the emotional impact:

- Nearly 60 percent of caregivers reported experiencing the onset of high to very high emotional stress, and nearly 40 percent reported experiencing physical stress
- 44 percent reported onset of anxiety
- 40 percent reported depression (compared to only 17 percent of non-caregiving peers)

The act of caregiving undoubtedly has a massive impact on quality of life for everyone involved. Writing about it as Beth did may seem like one more thing you don't have time for, but writing is a worthy friend to the grieving, often resulting in new thoughts and increased understanding. While it can be stressful, writing also helps you to connect to your emotions during difficult life events, especially when done with the intention to use it as a tool for your healing, as in the form of "expressive writing" suggested by Dr. James Pennebaker, a psychologist who was among the first to study the healing benefits of writing.[1] Emotional wellness benefits were found among grievers who dedicated fifteen to twenty minutes a day to free-flow (unedited) writing for four consecutive days on the same topic, and who wrote only for themselves, with no intention to share with others. The process helps you to acknowledge and examine your feelings and connect and process aspects of yourself you may not have yet uncovered. Not only can writing help you process your grief in real time, it may also be something you return to later to explore and edit or extrapolate into a form you do wish to share with others. Whether you choose to share your writing or not, the act of capturing the details may solidify a special moment in time in a form that may someday bring comfort to you and those invited to read your words, as Beth did on the eve of her transitioning her mother into a residential care facility. As she shared then:

"Tonight is my last night with my mom before she moves into her new home. We had a lovely family dinner with my parents, and then I helped Mum to bed. As usual, she was exhausted by the transition to nighttime and anxious as she lay in bed, trying to calm down from the hectic day. I held her hand, told her that I loved her, and assured her that I was here to help. She whispered, 'Thank you for helping me.' I responded, 'Of course! You helped me my whole life. You took great care of me as I grew up.' She broke into a huge smile and asked, 'I did?' I smiled again and said, 'Yes, you did. And it's my turn to take care of you.' As she shut her eyes for the night, she responded quietly, 'That makes me feel good.'

"Me too."

## HOW EMOTIONS ARE MADE

In reading about Beth and her mom, it is likely that you experienced some thoughts and feelings throughout the story. Maybe your emotions were stirred because you are also grieving a loved one to cognitive decline and can relate to Beth, or perhaps visions of your own aging loved one came to mind and Beth's story triggered worrisome thoughts about the future. Or maybe none of it resonated, and you felt nothing. No matter how you reacted, it's important to recognize what—if anything—came up for you. Being able to understand how and why you react to reading this story or any others, including your own, is an important bread crumb as you travel along your grief path. As you begin to work your way through the peaks and valleys of our second stop—feeling the stages of grief—being able to acknowledge and name your feelings will be key. The ability to understand them will take extra effort, but, in doing so, you will find yourself well able to navigate the detours and distractions ahead.

### *Who Is Driving?*

Picture this: you're driving the speed limit, your hands on the steering wheel at two and ten. You're focused on the road ahead of you and enjoying your drive when, suddenly, a car driving twenty miles over the speed limit comes out of nowhere and cuts you off, causing you to swerve. As you hit the brakes, you see them make a right-hand turn without signaling, nearly striking a pedestrian in the process. Most of us would call that driver names, perhaps paired with an accompanying rude hand gesture. But let's look more closely at why you might respond that way. Your response is probably due to fear, as you understood that their erratic, reckless driving could have caused an accident and caused harm. How is it that you were able to know that and react with your horn honk, hand gesture, or name-calling so quickly? Because of past experiences, social conditioning, and associations, we often react in a disproportionate or inappropriate manner. We react based in large part on how our brains are wired by the outcomes of past experiences, whether or not our prediction is founded in present truth. And often we react when we could, instead, assess and respond. If you could change the way you reacted toward that driver or a loved one who tested you, would you do it? Learning how and why you react is an important skill for ambiguous grievers. If we are truly committed to healing and to our own well-being, then we must first get comfortable with our emotions and feelings and sharpen our ability to recognize, understand, accept, and make peace with them when they greet (or ambush) us on our path.

## The Formulas of Feeling

Humans have been scribing about thoughts for nearly as long as we've been thinking. A recurring theme, extending as far back as the fourth century BC, is that of human emotions. Aristotle offered his ideas to the people of Ancient Greece in the work we know as the Rhetoric, in which he included his own list of emotions.[2] Since then, the quest for understanding emotion has continued, and in recent centuries has included notable offerings from naturalist Charles Darwin, psychiatrist Sigmund Freud, psychologist Robert Plutchik, neuroscientist Lisa Feldman Barrett, and researcher and storyteller Brené Brown, just to name a few. These contributions of ideas vary not only in concept (we're born with emotions, emotions are responses to external sources, etc.) but also in quantity: Aristotle lists fourteen emotions; Plutchik, eight; and Brown, eighty-seven. Paul Eckman has argued that only seven emotions are universal across age and culture. These "universal emotions" are anger, disgust, happiness, fear, sadness, surprise, and contempt.[3] If you dare to Google, you'll find the estimates extend up to a whopping 34,000 emotions! This massive range is credited not only to the confusing interchangeability between "emotions" and "feelings" but to the vast array of disciplines in pursuit of the cause. My therapist, Amy, helped me understand by explaining it this way: emotions are biological sensations that we have in response to things that we experience, while a feeling is an emotion with a thought attached to it. For example, how you feel about the emotion of surprise varies based on the thought attached to it; surprise may arise when you unexpectedly reunite with a dear old friend (delightful surprise) or unexpectedly discover a stranger in your home (dreadful surprise!). Surprise is the emotion, but the thought based on the experience creates the feeling: in this case, delight or dread. But depending on whom you ask about emotions—a theologian, sociologist, or philosopher, for example—the definitions, examples, and explanations will likely be widely divergent.

For the purpose of our journey, and in the spirit of simplicity, I'll use "feeling" and "emotion" interchangeably throughout this book unless otherwise specifically noted. More important to us than parsing the difference between an emotion and a feeling is being able to identify them correctly when they show up. To help you with that, I recommend a deeper exploration into the work of two authors who helped me, Brown and Plutchik. Recently, Brown published *Atlas of the Heart: Mapping Meaningful Connection and the Language of Human Experience*, a review of eighty-seven emotions that underscores the importance of language in helping us identify and express what we are feeling—a really helpful resource! Equally helpful is Plutchik's "Wheel of Emotions." This visual diagram, based on a color wheel, conceptualizes his findings. Plutchik maintained that nine emotions—the universal seven, plus anticipation and trust—serve as the base emotions from which all feelings are created.[4] Said another way: emotions are like primary colors, and feelings are the seemingly infinite number of hues created by mixing those primary colors. Just as shades of purple are created based on the different proportions of red combined with blue, our feelings can be created with a similar degree of variability. How intensely we feel something—or don't—is based on what we do with our emotions in any given situation.

In addition, Barrett, the author of *How Emotions Are Made: The Secret Life of the Brain*, has suggested that our emotions are not simply hardwired into us, but that they, too, are created, constructed in each moment via an ingredient list made up of core systems we organize as concepts.[5] These concepts direct our actions and produce meaning. In other words, emotions don't happen *to* us, they happen *by* us. Using this rationale, we can understand that we create our feelings and our emotions. This is helpful to know if we are going to improve our own ability to process grief and be of support to others who are grieving as well.

## CHANGE YOUR MIND, CHANGE YOUR EXPERIENCE

Catching a thought in real time can be tricky. We've evolved in large part due to our ability to assess a situation and quickly decide how to react. Our fight-or-flight response serves us well most of the time, especially when we are faced with a stimulus that threatens our sense of safety. Though we no longer face the same threats as our ancestors, this instinct is so deeply embedded in our consciousness that it's still activated and on full display today—like when we encounter derelict drivers or read an insulting comment on social media. In the same way, our minds hold deeply inscribed thoughts and feelings that are no longer true or applicable to the situation. The next time you recognize that you have a pattern of negatively reacting to something, take hold of your emotional wheel. Begin at your reaction and work backward to identify the old thought that started the chain reaction. Be prepared to find that the origin of the thought is likely rooted in your past or even your childhood, since knee-jerk reactions or behavior patterns are created by our past experiences. Isn't it exciting to know that we can help ourselves by assuming the role of a competent—albeit unsure—driver, instead of a passive and panicked passenger unwillingly along for the ride? Can you imagine how humanity might evolve if we collectively worked to rewire our brains in this way?

## Take the Wheel: Pre-Act

To apply this concept of rewiring, let's return to the derelict driver we encountered earlier. Our reflexive response was name-calling and rude gestures. What happens when we apply Feldman Barrett's theory and train ourselves to focus on how we ultimately created that response? What if, after they cut you off, your first thought was grounded in an intention to offer all drivers a grand assumption to think the very best of them instead? Brené Brown describes this as "assuming positive intent," which gives "the most generous interpretation possible to the intentions, words, and actions of others."[6] Applying this, your thought might instead be, "That driver must be having an emergency and need to be somewhere urgently to be driving like that." If that's a stretch for you—because, let's face it, some drivers are consistently terrible—consider practicing a mediocre assumption. In a less grand assumption, your thought might say, "That is one awful driver, and there are probably reasons they shouldn't be behind the wheel." With these thoughts, you may feel less that they are trying to harm you, and your mind could then seek to assign a feeling commensurate with the thought—possibly compassion or empathy, or, at the least, neutrality. In turn, the feeling you generate could then prompt a reaction likely rooted in love or indifference; you might say a prayer for the driver's safety and for those sharing the same road, or shake your head and continue on about your day. In both instances, your response is then to continue on peacefully, not brooding in hostility or, worse, reacting with road rage. In changing your thought before the feeling is attached, you have directed the outcome. I think of this as "pre-action," an intervention of thought that seeks to produce a desired re-action. Try it!

---

### Exercise 7 | Pre-Act

Think of a scenario that causes a reaction in you that you would like to change. This can be a direct interaction with the loved one you are grieving, a secondary person playing a part in your grief story, or a situation that triggers you. Work through the following prompts in your journal.

Describe the situation: _____

_____

What were you thinking? _____

What were you feeling? _____

How do you react? _____

What is a grand assumption you might have offered

in this situation? _____

PRE-ACT! Now, consider the situation again. When

viewing it through the lens of a grand assumption,

what might your thoughts reflect (remember to

gift the grand assumption)? _____

What might you be feeling? _____

How might you respond? _____

## Bonus Questions for Seasoned Travelers

Can you recall a time you felt this way before?
Can you recall a time you thought this way before?
What patterns do you notice?

Continue to complete this exercise and apply it with reactions you want to change. Remember that you are working on altering only your own reactions, because you are not all-powerful and (spoiler!) do not have the ability to change anyone but yourself. It will take some practice, but with sustained effort, you just might find that this powerful tool helps you grow through your grief. At the very least, it presents an incredible opportunity to transform not only your pain, but the remainder of your human experience as well.

_____

## BRAIN CHANGE AT ANY AGE

While dementia-related diagnoses like Alzheimer's affect the elderly, another form of cognitive change, traumatic brain injury (TBI), is a prevalent diagnosis in adolescent and young adult populations. The leading causes of moderate to severe TBI in the United States are unintentional falls and motor vehicle accidents. Unlike the slow reveal of symptoms often seen in dementia patients, the TBI patient and their family often experience this change suddenly and unexpectedly. If the impairment from the accident doesn't reveal itself immediately, it becomes evident quickly, since TBI injury impacts behavior, mood, temper, reasoning, executive function, and more. Sometimes, however, a TBI is sustained without awareness, and its impact isn't discovered until changes are glaringly evident.

There are an estimated 2.8 million TBI-related hospitalizations each year in the United States alone, and 43 percent of those affected are discharged with a long-term disability. Add in those afflicted with a minor traumatic brain injury, such as a concussion, and the numbers skyrocket to nearly 60 million cases globally each year. Whether the traumatic brain injury is mild or severe, the Centers for Disease Control recently reported that the populations with the highest prevalence of TBI continue to be young adults and the elderly. Relatedly, they found that such injury creates significant changes in family structure and persistent adverse effects on caregivers, similar to those impacted by Alzheimer's.

## ASSUMPTIONS IN GRIEF

The feelings experienced throughout the stages of grief are often powerful, unpredictable, and even frustrating. During our first therapy session, Amy warned that the coming weeks were going to be undeniably difficult. Not only would she be helping me process the details surrounding my discovery, she would work to help me navigate the stages of grief she told me to expect. Even though I had no reason to doubt her, I hoped she was wrong—that I would be spared what sounded like a brewing emotional storm system carrying a deluge of difficult feelings.

We're all likely familiar with the stages of grief: they are, again, anger, denial, bargaining, depression, acceptance, and meaning. Amy clarified that my experience of the stages wasn't guaranteed, but highly likely. I was dubious, but she'd been practicing for twenty years, and I understood she was trying to prepare me for impending emotional annihilation. "The question is not *if* loss will bring about these feelings," she said. "It's how will you cope, how intense will each be, how long will each stay, and what tools can we equip you with so that you can experience these feelings and process your grief in a healthy way?"

The first few sessions were intense and overwhelming, oscillating between disclosing the painful details of my discovery and regaling her with happy stories from our recent family vacation. I outlined to her my strategy for what was next: getting support for my three heartbroken children and a soon-to-be-former husband. I had my act together and did not have time to waste feeling depressed. By my fourth session in as many days, we were underway in building our therapist-patient relationship. The way Amy listened and reflected my words back to me felt validating, like she really understood me.

"I hear you; your family is in crisis, and you are feeling like you don't have time to be depressed because they need you. It's understandable you feel that way," she said before redirecting our productive chat. "But we've got to focus on you, on what you're going through, about your needs right now. Do you have any family or friends who can come for a week or so to help out?" I shook my head, indicating that I didn't understand her question. *Why was she asking me this? How was this helpful?*

Amy went on to describe distressing feelings that I wasn't even having. As she did, it became clear that I was her student in a crash course on emotional disaster preparedness. She looked at me like a parent copping to the truth about Santa Claus, delivering the devastating truth and wishing they weren't the messenger.

"Such a blindside fractures the ego," she began. "You're

unpacking a lot here. And I'm concerned that as you begin to process it all—the betrayal, the loss—it will likely be just too much for you to carry. It would be too much for anyone."

I stared, unable to digest her words as she reached to a side table and grabbed a box of tissues.

Holding it up with both hands, she began, "Think of your mind like this box. When we are presented with information to process that is within the space of our box, we know what to do with it." Amy's left hand pointed inside the space, and I nodded in understanding.

"Inside is normal. But"—she pointed to the empty air beside the box—"when something happens outside of this space"—her free hand stirred the empty air—"then the brain has a different job to do. It has to process something unexpected and something it doesn't understand. Something like this is far outside of your 'normal' experience, and isn't something you simply will your way through."

My ears started ringing. Amy tried another approach, pointing again to the area outside of the tissue-brain box. "Your experience happened over here, outside of normal. That's considered a trauma. Do you understand?" The word hung between us, suspended in some sort of stop-motion animation: *traaaauuuummmmaa.*

Amy said, "Processing what happened and processing your grief are two different and two very intense experiences. Your brain is going to be doing a lot of thinking, and your body will be undergoing a lot of feeling, Steph."

My attention went to the ringing in my ears, now reaching a crescendo. Amy noticed my discomfort and stopped talking. "You okay?"

I nodded yes, even though we both knew that I was decidedly not okay.

I wasn't okay when I sat down for our session, and I certainly wasn't okay as I digested what she was saying: that my discovery was something so unexpected that it was outside the space of the tissue box, and my mind would likely need a long time and take great effort to process it. What I *could* process right away was that Amy was bumming me out. I had assumed I would feel better talking with her—after all, therapists were supposed to be helpful. But so far Amy was proving to be anything but.

"You said you aren't sleeping. Would you like to talk about some mild prescriptions that may help you through this? An anti-anxiety or low-dose antidepressant?" Amy's eyes implored me to say yes, but I didn't comply.

Instead, I snapped. "Anxiety? Maybe. But depression? Depression!?" I realized Amy only knew me as I had showed up in her office days before, shaking and shattered. She didn't know *Me*; hardworking, determined, and raised with the family-first Midwestern values that ingrained a can-do, get-it-done attitude that detested wallowing. "No, no, no. That's not for me. I mean, I'm not anti-medicine—I take ibuprofen, even Advil PM (as needed)," I confessed, "and a multivitamin, some supplements. But that's really it. That's all I need."

Her face shifted into neutral. I couldn't read her response, and, uncomfortable with the silence, I pressed on, bullet-pointing my bio to help Amy fill in the blanks she obviously needed filled. "I've actually trained others on mindset and how to develop mental fortitude." Cutting her some slack, I went on, "You wouldn't know this of course, especially based on how I look right now, but I've always been someone who has my shit together. Some of my best friends tease me about being a unicorn, all rainbows and cupcakes, because I'm such an optimist, especially during the hard stuff." She was unmoved by my testimony, her blank expression now solidly parked. My closing argument would need to be strong and decisive.

"I've run several marathons, Amy." This was an invitation for her to join me in understanding. But even with that unde-niable evidence, Amy responded with a shrug.

"That's an impressive accomplishment, Steph, but I'm afraid that won't be much help to you right now. Processing grief and trauma isn't about endurance or positive think-ing. It's much different. It's a long-term stress on the nervous system."

Unbelievable. If her annoying redirection and focus on me (and not the actual problem) weren't enough, now she was pushing pills and prognosticating PTSD—as if things could get any worse.

Not helpful, Amy.

I rose from the couch and collected my coat and purse. Amy looked up at the clock on the wall, confused. Before she could remind me that we still had twenty minutes left, I answered her initial question, punctuating my words with a sharp tongue and defiant tone that my thirteen-year-old self would have been proud of. "No. I don't want to be medicated. I don't need to be medicated." I hastily opened the door to leave and paused, turning to face her. The middle-school mean girl I had long outgrown suddenly reappeared. My eyes narrowed, my finger wagged, and, my voice petulant, I said, "You don't know me, Amy." I marched my offended heart and bruised ego right out of her office and didn't look back.

Hours later, embarrassed by my immature behavior, I contacted Amy to apologize. The truth was that I felt wounded by the reality of my situation and I was fearful of all the unknowns. In retrospect, I realized that even though I'd only had a handful of sessions with her, she knew more than I did about what was ahead of me. With hours of therapy accrued since then, I now understand that my reaction was also rooted in my own false narrative—an assumption that Amy thought I was weak and was not of sound mind to navigate the impending trauma tornado. Or, perhaps, she didn't know what to do to help me, so was punting to pharma instead. That inaccurate belief, coupled with my lack of previous experience with antidepressants, created a fearful defiance. The reality was that I was afraid taking the meds might somehow intercept my ability to reason clearly, cloud my judgment, or, worse, minimize or even numb what I was feeling. I feared that any of those outcomes could endanger my mental acumen at a time when I needed every neuron.

Still, even after I had apologized for my juvenile behavior and sat again for another session, I deemed the introduction of prescription medications a greater risk than reward and declined Amy's offer when she floated it once more at the end of our hour. "Are you sure, Steph? Just something to help you get some sleep?" I had nighttime ibuprofen at home and told her I'd lean on that if it came to it. It seemed like Amy wasn't hearing me—but what happened within the coming weeks proved the exact opposite: it was me who wasn't hearing her. As it turned out, what came next changed the trajectory of my relationship, my year ahead, and so much more. And though I didn't realize it at the time, my reaction in Amy's office was a big clue to finding the buried treasure that held the tools to my healing.

### Feeling Your Feelings

Though I didn't agree with or understand some of what Amy was telling me, I was clear on one particular point: it was of utmost importance to allow myself to have all of the feelings— meaning I had to experience them and accept them, not resist them. As a deeply feeling person already, I had learned from a young age that sitting in my feelings helped me understand myself and others. For me, "sitting in my feelings" means I tune in to my heart and allow my body to act as an interpreter to what I'm feeling. Sometimes this looks like gentle walking, sitting still, or chair rocking, and sometimes it looks like a child having a temper tantrum on the closet floor.

But even as you allow yourself space to feel, and your heart and body work to entertain whichever feeling has emerged, your mind will often continue to chime in, too—and for me, that was not at all helpful. Instead, I'd visit the past, replaying bittersweet memories, or I'd project into the future, viewing snippets of memories that will never be, like celebrating a fiftieth wedding anniversary or that incredible dream vacation we'd planned. If you also experience too much "help" from the mind in this way, it can lead to wallowing or worse, as it did for me. Ultimately, all of our emotions demand to be heard and all of our feelings need to be expressed. Whether they come out in a healthy manner as they happen, or break through years later, spiked, sideways, and impaling others, is up to you. Elizabeth Lesser, author of *The Seeker's Guide: Making Your Life a Spiritual Adventure*, articulates this so well. She writes:

"If we do not suffer a loss all the way to the end, it will wait for us. It won't just dissipate and disappear. Rather, it will fester, and we will experience its sorrow later, in stranger forms."

*Exercise 8 | Feeling Formulas in Grief*

When Amy asked if I'd like to begin antidepressant medication, I felt offended. The feeling formula was likely something like this:

A heavy dose of fear + a generous addition of shame + a pinch of embarrassment + a sprinkle of anxiety

Apply an experience in your own grief to create your own feeling formula. This can help you gain insight to how and why you react.

Describe a time you reacted in a way you later regretted.

What are the feelings that came up for you during this interaction?

Rank them in order, from the one you felt the most to the one you felt the least, and use this to construct your feeling formula. The goal is to be better able to understand what we are feeling, and why, so that we can respond thoughtfully from a place of peace and not unconsciously react out of fear.

Here's an example. In my interaction with Amy, I can identify four feelings that I experienced as I made my decision to leave the session: shame, embarrassment, anxiety, and fear. In ranked order, fear was the biggest, followed by shame. I was also feeling embarrassed, which in turn added some feeling of anxiety.

---

*Traveler's Tip: Managing Your Mind*

By weaving new thoughts around our distressing circumstances, we can consciously reconstruct our feelings to
serve us, instead of being at the whim of our unconscious
feelings. This doesn't mean we are seeking to eliminate our
feelings or not experience them, nor that the waves of emotion will cease. As we navigate the changing tides of our
loss, having the ability to re-create our feelings empowers
us to manage their intensity and duration, turning a tsu-
nami into a light rain. The more we harness our thoughts,
the clearer we can show up for ourselves, and the more
confidently we can take on the swells we encounter as we
ride the waves of grief.

---

# WE'VE GOT COMPANY:
# ENTERTAINING THE STAGES OF GRIEF

As if on cue, the stages of grief unleashed their attack, and
just as Amy predicted, I was soon besieged by the emotional
missiles she had warned about. My thoughts, emotions, and
feelings were an unorganized, undisciplined mob living
inside my mind, which I now realize was understandable—in
the aftermath of an activating event, particularly one involving trauma, it takes time and energy to digest and apply new
learning, especially as you take on grief. For me, this happened
when the initial shock of my activating event began to recede,

stripping away my trauma-induced shell of armor. This left me exposed and vulnerable to an onslaught of errant emotions and frenetic feelings at an intensity I had never experienced. Grief's well-planned attack commenced three weeks after my discovery, when Denial was deployed, reporting, "This doesn't make sense. You are blowing this out of proportion. Don't be so dramatic."

But my gut told me this was untrue. Denial soon retreated, and red-hot Anger rained down: "What the hell!? Who does this? I don't deserve this!" There was a lot of scream-sobbing during this campaign. When I threw our wedding photo across the room (not my best moment), I felt out of control and at the mercy of my captor. Anger demanded to be witnessed, refusing to leave until I obliged. So began the daily drills of wailing, pillow punching, whisper-yelling, and sustained and unrelenting verbal attacks directed at the ghosts around me. These stages rotated unpredictably, with no break in their around-the-clock campaign. Bargaining often took over to work the night shift and kept me busy when I should have been sleeping.

Exhausted from Anger, I'd lie in bed and engage with Bargaining for hours. Most times, this looked like establishing an "if-then" narrative, which calmed and collected the madness in my mind: *If I could just understand, then I could consider alternatives to divorce.* If there was a way to fix this—to find out the "why"—then I could certainly put my life back together again. *If not me, then who?* I felt this deep within my soul. Bargaining proved to be more of a problem-solver than a soldier and became my ally, working to help me develop my own insurgence. In the War Room of my mind, we'd whiteboard ideas to fix my pain. *Okay, how about this! Resume normal activities, like regular dinners or watching shows together. This way you'll be able to tease out what else you need to know and can figure out what help is needed.* Under the spell of Bargaining, such plans were brilliant in the War Room, but failed on the battlefield of daily life. Reinstating date night or watching an episode of reality TV would do nothing but worsen my own life. In reality, Bargaining had distracted me with false narratives and wasn't an ally after all. For fleeting moments in between the Anger, Denial, and Bargaining, I would feel a brief reprieve of Acceptance. Though it came only after complete emotional depletion and its stay was fleeting, it afforded me a mental clarity and a welcome rest from the exhausting nature of the other stages. My experience of acceptance was actually more of a dressed-up version of apathy, but it allowed me space to tune in to something else. It felt like a stage, but it was different than the others Amy had talked to me about. Though I wasn't able to name it, I could recognize when it took charge.

Looking back, it's both funny and sad. I was desperately grasping for anything that could repair the nuclear-disaster-level damage sustained by my marriage. At this point, it had been over a month and, still, only my friend Steph and Amy knew the full truth. I just wanted to put my family back together again before anyone noticed something was wrong. Meanwhile, I was falling apart, unable to reconcile what I had learned with what I thought I knew without a doubt. If I was so wrong on something that I would have bet my life on, what else was I wrong about? Betrayal trauma is like that; a special kind of hell that not only fractures the relationship between loved ones, but also fractures the sense of self of the betrayed, their trust of the world, and their sense of personal safety within it.

## Everything Hurts

Six weeks after my activating event, Depression arrived and took me captive. Everything around me shifted, including my breath; each inhalation a stunted, sodden mix of stagnant air and hot tears, each exhale shallow and shivering. Depression's grasp prevented me from taking full breaths. It had wrapped itself onto me, adhering like a space alien to a human host, assimilating me. Aware of the transformation, I lay in the darkness and awaited the next move, drinking gulps of air every time I noticed I wasn't breathing.

I steadied myself in anticipation. As my mind offered the suggestion that I was having a heart attack, I found my breath. Gasping, dizzy, and disoriented, I needed water, but with no energy to venture to the kitchen to get it myself, I lay motionless staring at the ceiling above. I focused on the unmoving ceiling fan. It hadn't worked reliably in months, but I wondered what would happen if I turned it on high speed and resumed my place under its blades. How long would it take to wobble its way off the ceiling and fall down on me? How badly would it injure me? Would it be enough to admit me to the hospital, where a kind and loving medical team would bring me water and nurse me back to health? As I fantasized about this, I realized I had just moments prior diagnosed myself with a heart attack. Maybe I should have called an ambulance, but I texted Amy's emergency number instead. After answering her questions, which included my family heart history, she asked if I'd ever had a panic attack, which was a common, stress-induced physiological response, and appropriate given all that I was going through.

As I lay in bed, my thoughts pivoted to processing my reality. My marriage was beyond repair, I didn't know what—if anything—about my marriage had been real, and I didn't know what my future was going to be now that the one I had envisioned had been ripped away. I startled myself by speaking up. "I know who I am," my own voice murmured. "I know who I am." I spoke again, this time as a declaration. I didn't know the past or the future, and I didn't know why this had happened or how I would get through it. But my soul did, and in that moment, I recognized its truth. Although it didn't solve anything that night, I clung to it, because it felt like the only truth I had.

*Exercise 9 | Your Stages of Grief*

Take a look at the onset of your grief and examine your feelings as you experienced each stage. Try to identify examples of when you have felt each stage and note what feelings emerged for you.

- Denial
- Anger
- Bargaining
- Depression
- Acceptance (Note: I didn't feel acceptance for a long time. I recognize that acceptance came for me when I began to practice meditation and mindfulness, which calmed and collected my mind and allowed me to feel peace again.)
- Any other stages or extended periods of a particular feeling you experienced (e.g., meaning, confusion, etc.)

## ROCK-BOTTOM RUBBLE

Three weeks into a debilitating depression and nine weeks since the discovery, I desperately wanted to feel better—or to feel anything. I was barely able to tend to my children, and the mounting stack of dishes in my sink was a daily reminder that I needed help at home. Still the only two who knew the full truth, Steph and Amy, both encouraged me to tell others how and why

I was struggling. I knew they were right, and so, after a particularly empowering pep talk from Steph, I finally deployed distress flares via text message to a few trusted friends and friend groups. I made brief phone calls to my family. The message was the same for everyone: I relayed simply that I was divorcing, devastated and drowning after the discovery of affairs. My girlfriends organized themselves and initiated an impromptu rescue operation that included an impressive twelve-week stretch of actual boots-on-the-ground support. Along with my family, they arrived from six different states and took turns caring for my kids, our home, and me. They walked our dog, drove carpools, folded laundry, grocery shopped, cooked meals, paid bills, and checked homework. They played countless hands of Uno with the kids and sat with me in silent support over jigsaw puzzles, a soothing activity for my overactive brain. They set timers to be sure I was drinking water, and they brushed my hair. They mothered the hell out of us all, while I continued to ride the roller coaster of my ongoing grief.

During the week my friend Carrie was visiting, Depression was still acting as general, large and in charge directing the troops. As Carrie unloaded groceries, she mentioned she was surprised I had turned down anxiety meds. "If not now, then when?" she asked. In our thirty years of friendship, we had a long history of direct, loving truth-telling between us. We relied on one another as sounding boards and mirrors, to listen without judgment and point out blind spots as only a trusted advisor can. While I was brushing my teeth and pondering her question that evening, the reflection in my mirror stopped me. I somehow managed to look both gaunt and swollen at the same time. I had lost nearly twenty pounds, revealing cheekbones I hadn't seen in as many years, while my eyes, now perpetually wet and strewn with bursting red vessels, protruded from their sockets. I looked like a real-life caricature drawing. My skin was flaking, and my hair was falling out in clumps on the rare occasion I had the energy to wash it. I was a shell of my former self, both physically and mentally. *If not now, then when?* I questioned my reflection. Though my gut instinct had been that antidepressants weren't the answer, I didn't know what was and had no other reasonable offers to consider. Awake through the night, I acknowledged yet another painful truth: I couldn't trust my gut. It had flickered nary a warning during the decade I was being duped, so why should I follow it now, after it had failed me so miserably? The next day, Carrie drove me to my appointment with Amy, where, white flag waving, I promptly asked for a prescription. "Yes, of course!" Amy was noticeably glad, her relief palpable. "I've been waiting for this, Steph. There is nothing to feel bad about," she said assuredly. "This is going to help you, I promise."

### Surrender

Overnight, my neatly decorated nightstand transformed into a bedside apothecary. Looking at the bottles filled with pills to help me sleep, stifle my panic attacks, and relieve my depression, I felt a mix of shame and relief. Had I accepted the parachute of a prescription sooner, I would likely have had a softer landing into the awful stage of depression the night it arrived. Weeks later, I was relieved to feel that the medications hadn't done what I had feared; I still had my cognition, and, to both my delight and disdain, my reasoning abilities had not dulled. The medications hadn't changed my thinking, but instead had helped to quiet the chatter in my overworked brain. As the antidepressants began to kick in, I received their first gift: a full eight hours of sleep, something that had eluded me for months since my chaotic mind had been working around the clock. Like a desperate detective obsessed with a cold case, my mind had been examining memories and moments for any missed clues, tracking every mental lead as far as possible, each leading me down dark and disturbing paths, and each ending in dead ends offering only more unanswered questions. Ultimately, the only things I learned from this were (1) that the game of mental Matlock was unhelpful to every part of me, body and soul, and (2) dissecting the past was a futile exercise. My mind needed to be in the present moment.

---

*Traveler's Tip: Medication Is a Personal Decision*

- Prescription medication is not one-size-fits-all and is certainly not a cure-all. (What worked for a friend, for example, didn't work for me.)

- Talk with your doctor to learn if medication might be an option for you. (I did—it was!)
- Communicate with your doctor about possible side effects and to ensure your medications are managed appropriately. (Don't attempt this on your own—leave it to the professionals.)
- It's common to stop, start, and switch medications before finding what combination provides the most support. (It took three rounds for me!)
- Titrating dosages or changing a medication altogether can be frustrating, so prepare to be patient through the process.
- Remember that medication can be a support when needed but doesn't need to be forever. Your doctor will guide you through the weaning process when you are ready. (For me, that was about eighteen months on, with one month of weaning off.)
- Along the way, ask yourself: Am I noticing improvements? Am I feeling worse? Is this thing on?

## MINDFULNESS AND MEDITATION

"When you pick up your tea, you may like to breathe in in order to bring your mind back to your body, and become completely fully present in the here and now. I don't think of the past anymore, I don't think of the future anymore, I am free from the past, from the future, and there

is a real encounter between me and the tea. And
peace, happiness, and joy is possible during the
time I drink my tea."

—THICH NHAT HANH[7]

Since the experience of ambiguous grief is a result of loss,
lingering in the past with your mind in "memory-mode" can
be counterproductive to your healing. But if you discipline
your mind around this awareness, you can change your focus
and find peace. One way to do this is to learn how to move
out of remembering and into the present moment. This isn't
a new idea, so you've probably heard about it somewhere
along your journey. Given that, it's likely that you are in one
of three groups: those who are not the least interested in this
section and are skimming ahead, those who are curious to
learn more and have highlighters ready, and those who are
a combination of both, skeptical but cautiously willing to
give it a try. Perhaps you have already leveraged these tools,
or like me, a cautious skeptic, you are only peripherally
aware of them but haven't had use for such tools until now. I
understand. Amy had encouraged me to try meditation, but,
much like I did with her suggestion of medication, I rejected
it. My belief was that (1) I didn't have time, and (2) I didn't
think I could "do" it. I didn't know anything about meditation and later realized that my lack of exposure, mixed with
unfounded thoughts that I had assigned to the idea, had kept
me from experiencing what it meant to meditate. For some
people experiencing grief, being still and alone in meditation

feels like a vulnerable act, because without something to keep busy, we are confronted with difficult feelings surrounding our loved one and our loss. It's not uncommon to adopt externally sourced coping strategies (like shopping, working, drinking, eating, exercising, etc.) as a mechanism to protect us from what we fear may arise in the quiet of our minds.

For some, like me, mindfulness and meditation felt counterintuitive. My life was drastically changing in real time, with much happening at every stage of grief. I was using my brain to understand and find solutions to the urgent problems in my life, so I thought that taking time to sit and do nothing was the epitome of counterproductive activity. My thought was wrong (again!).

The concepts of mindfulness and the practice of meditation have gained popularity in the past decade, becoming especially prominent shortly after the onset of the COVID-19 pandemic. However, these are far from new practices. In fact, they're powerful stress-management tools that have been used for millennia. Though the terms are often used interchangeably, they are not the same. While there are varying definitions available, here are the ones I use: Mindfulness is bringing your awareness to the present moment, without judgment, anytime, anywhere. Meditation is an act that you practice during which you dedicate time and space to focused attention. You can also think of it like a subset, in the same way that not all Christians are Catholic, but all Catholics are Christians. When we meditate, we are practicing mindfulness, but when practicing mindfulness, we are not confined only to the act of meditation. One of the shared benefits of both is stress reduction, and as you likely know by now, stress is exacerbated during traumatic events, significant loss, and grief. This is why we're adding these time-tested tools to our ambiguous griever's backpack.

Only hours after I had snubbed Amy's meditation suggestion, a perfectly timed episode of *Super Soul Sunday* changed my thinking. The topic was mindfulness, and Eckhart Tolle, author and thought leader, was being interviewed by Oprah Winfrey. Tolle spoke about his work and the importance of focusing attention on life in the present moment. I didn't know it then, but my soul self was signaling me, rousing me to attention. Instinctively, I took out a notebook, started the episode over and began to take notes like a student on the first day of class. "So, when you listen to a thought, you are aware not only of the thought, but also of yourself as the witness to the thought. The moment you start watching the thinker, a higher level of consciousness becomes activated within you," Tolle said. My new professor had blown my mind. In under an hour, I had been introduced to a new way of thinking and had become inspired to learn more about mindfulness and meditating.

My first attempt at meditation was a failure. I used the Headspace app, and though the sequence I attempted was just ten minutes, it felt like sixty. I considered the notes I'd taken from Tolle; they were a source of encouragement, so I persisted. However, the act felt foreign to me for several weeks. Stepping away from the chaos within seemed both futile and counterintuitive to my typically busy mind. As Andy, the Aussie guide on Headspace, had coached me through the act of meditation, though, so, too, my breath guided my heart. I coached my heart rate down from a sprint, to a run, to a jog, to a walk, to a stroll. The static faded, and my mind tuned in to the frequency it had been seeking, the one Amy and Eckhart knew was helpful to us humans with busy minds. My mind—not me—observed the breath moving into my lungs, the exhale out of my nose, and the sound of the air as it circulated. It noticed my breath in partnership with my strolling heartbeat. Meditation was also good for my body.

Soon, I began the practice of present awareness in the regular moments of my day. While sweeping the floor, I focused on the movement of the broom, the stretch of my arms, the collection of dust on the floor. While cooking dinner, I focused on the chopping sound, the brightly colored vegetables, the smell of simmering soup. I think of mindfulness as closing the dozen open tabs in the browser of my mind and leaving only one open. In that way, I am not multitasking or moving through an activity unconsciously. I am consciously aware of the present moment and my interaction within it. A concept that helped me develop my practice is one that may help you, too. Think of the thoughts of your mind like they are a small child; always asking questions, reporting observations, and incessantly making noise. When you need to quiet a small child, giving them a task will do the trick! Ask them to count breaths or repeat a mantra to help keep them focused and quiet and allow you moments of peace.

To help understand and observe the difference between you and your thoughts, consider assigning a name to your Mind Child—that is, who you hear chattering even as you read this.

You are *not* the Mind Child; you are the observer who is aware of the Mind Child. I refer to my chatterer as "Dear One." Dear One is always talking, and so, when I need to, I greet her with empathy and gratitude, and then I kindly ask her to shut up.

When "hard" emotions and feelings visited, I could turn to my mindfulness practice to lower the barometer of intensity. The same was true for my daily meditation practice, which became my most anticipated time of day. I was intentional as to when I would practice and enlisted support from my children to honor my privacy while I was having this important time. My ten minutes grew to twenty and became a cherished part of my afternoon, and remain so today.

Just as we have discovered that our ancestors have been deeply pondering human emotion for thousands of years, it is widely recognized that mindfulness and meditation have been practiced equally as long, if not longer, as part of religious teachings around the world—Buddhist, Hindu, and Christian alike encourage them as a daily discipline for the great many benefits they bring.

## Real Benefits

Though the benefits have been known and celebrated for millennia, best estimates indicate that only 6.25 percent of the global population practices mindfulness and meditation. Currently only a meager 14 percent of U.S. residents report that they have tried to meditate at least once. Perhaps the low number in the United States is due to a misconception that mindfulness and meditation are faith-based, Buddhist, "anti-Christian," or even paganistic. Their Eastern origins and subsequent teaching took centuries to spread and only grew into mainstream American awareness in the last fifty years. But thanks in part to a global pandemic in 2020 and additional rising stress factors, these practices have gained popularity—and they have massive benefits. Studies by Massachusetts General Hospital and the Harvard Medical School have discovered impressive physiological changes in the brains of people who used the meditation technique of mind-body stress reduction for just thirty minutes a day over eight weeks. Those changes include:

Increased self-confidence and focus (thickened posterior angulate)

Increased ability to regulate emotions, learn, and remember (thickened left hippocampus)

Increased empathy, compassion, and perspective (thickened temporoparietal junction)

Decreased stress and reduced triggering of the fight-or-flight response (reduced size of the amygdala)

All for a mere twenty-eight hours over the span of fifty-six days (that's just 2 percent of your day)!

## Mind Over (Gray) Matter

"Another way to look at meditation is to view the process of thinking itself as a waterfall, a continual cascading of thought. In cultivating mindfulness, we are going beyond or behind our thinking, much the way you might find a vantage point in a cave or depression in the rock behind a waterfall. We still see and hear the water, but we are out of the torrent."[8]

—JON KABAT-ZINN

Another surprising benefit of mindfulness and meditation has been proven by research. A team of collaborating researchers from the University of Massachusetts Medical School, Massachusetts General Hospital, and Germany's Bender Institute of Neuroimaging examined MRI images of individuals who meditate regularly and made some interesting discoveries. The images determined that these practices have a profound long-term effect: they increase gray-matter density in our brains (the stuff that affects memory, learning, motor function, and more), and not only slow the process of aging in the brain, but actually *reverse* it.[9]

Harvard neuroscientist Sara Lazar,[10] who was involved with the study, said: "It's well documented that our cortex shrinks as we get older—it's harder to figure things out and remember things. But in this one region, 50-year-old meditators had the same amount of gray matter as 25-year-olds." Furthermore, the gray matter wasn't simply "already there"—proof that we can use meditation like seeds to regrow our gray matter.[11]

Whether we are battling difficult memories of our lost loved one, triggered by distracted drivers, fretting about the future, or stressed over our overwhelming responsibilities, the myriad of mind invaders we encounter every day is a part of being human. The sooner we can come to understand that we are not the thoughts in our minds, the sooner we can discover our own consciousness and our innate peace.

While it is hard work to rewire our reactions, overcome difficult feelings, update our thoughts, and sit in stillness, science shows us that it is more than possible and that doing so can impact our wellness in many ways. We can be the boss of our minds.

---

*Exercise 10 | Press Pause—Meditate in Loving Kindness*

As you practice meditation, remember that it's okay when your mind wanders (and it will). Meditation is not the absence of thought, but rather the observation of thought. It is the practice of quieting your mind and experiencing the present moment. When your Mind Child begins to chatter, simply shush it and return to your chosen focus (breath, mantra, etc.). For this meditation, try sending kindness to the loved one you are grieving. If that is too difficult, send kindness to yourself.

1. Find a quiet space.
2. Set a timer for 5 minutes.
3. Ideally, sit comfortably in a chair with your back erect, feet flat on the floor.
4. Rest your hands in your lap.
5. Deeply inhale 3 counts, pause 1 count, slowly exhale 3 counts. As you breathe, picture your loved one (or yourself) and send them kindness and love, visualizing a golden light extending from your soul to theirs.
6. Repeat until 5 minutes have passed.

Reflect on that experience by answering the following questions. Revisit these questions monthly to monitor your own growth and assess how meditation is most beneficial to you.

What did you feel in your body while meditating?

What thoughts came up for you while meditating?

Did you make any discoveries or connections during your meditation?

Just like learning to ride a bike, meditation is something that takes practice and persistence, but once you find your balance, it's a vehicle that carries you faster and farther than before, and with extended health benefits, too. Though you may experience times in your life when you aren't using this mode of transport as much as you once were, you can always begin again. Learning it once will serve you as long as you live.

## WHAT IS THAT?

Just as we know it's beneficial to accept and not to resist feeling our emotions, emerging research tells us that labeling an emotion or putting one's feelings into words can actually help to regulate their effect. Psychologist Dan Siegel refers to this practice as "name it to tame it," and in *The Whole-Brain Child*, a book he co-authored with Tina Payne Bryson, he explains that naming an emotion generated in the right side of the brain engages the left side, which allows the brain to make sense of the feeling and experience a sense of control.

This is yet another reason for you to practice welcoming and getting to know your emotions as they occur. For me and others who have shared their experience of grief, it is clear that medication can be a helpful resource, but it is in no way a cure-all. As I understood this, I sought other modalities that would also help me process the many emotions and intense feelings of my grief, long after I started and later stopped taking antidepressants. The continued act of observing my mind and scanning my body became second nature and helped me locate and correctly identify joy as well as other feelings. Tuning in to my body for physical clues helped me to name these visitors. For example, I noticed a dizzy sensation often accompanied the feeling of anxiety, and the sensation of suffocation usually escorted the feeling of helplessness. Some of these visitors were far more complex and harder to pinpoint, since they were made up of subtle nuance with shared or overlapping traits.

After a few months of practice tuning in to my body, I had gotten pretty good at it—with one exception. A particular feeling eluded me to the point of frustration, especially as it began to visit with more frequency. As with seeing the face of an old friend but not being able to recall their name, my frustration grew each time it would arrive and leave unidentified. The name of this mystery guest was on the tip of my tongue, yet something in my mind was blocking my ability to reveal it. After several months, the only clues I could isolate were: (1) it was a familiar feeling, something I knew I had encountered both before and after my activating event; (2) it was more "neutral" than "good" or "bad" (though we know all feelings are neutral—it's the thoughts we assign to them that control our perception); and (3) it did not adhere to a pattern or result from a known trigger. I set an intention to acknowledge this feeling as it arrived, but to pay it no more attention beyond that. I believed that it would come to me eventually, just like those escaped names always seem to. I stopped searching my mind for the answer and, encouraged by the early benefits from my practice of body scanning, soon decided to turn my mind off and sharpen my newly introduced tools of mindfulness and meditation.

I didn't know it then, but mindfulness and meditation proved to be the perfect training partner to my newfound efforts to pinpoint and name my feelings. While both helped me tune in to the present moment, mindfulness sensitized my awareness of the world around me and meditation heightened my internal attention. Together, this created a satisfying effect, similar to the feelings experienced after a day of intense closet cleaning—where clearing your space leaves it, and you, feeling organized and lighter. But just like a freshly purged closet, you'll be able to easily find what you're looking for only if you maintain the new order of your space, which, thankfully, takes just a few minutes each day.

In daily meditation, I was able to keep up with my closet and learned to tune out the "me of the world" and (re)connect to my soul self, that constant part of me that had always been there—at the Rotor ride on my sixth birthday, on the vomitous floor that terrible Tuesday, and in every single second in between. But reconnecting to this part of me wasn't easy, because I felt that my soul self had betrayed me, too. Essentially, because it had failed to alert me to something amiss in my marriage, I no longer considered that part of myself to be a reliable resource. But that began to change after a few months of intentionally naming my feelings and reconnecting with myself through meditation. The benefits of both converged, and I found that my soul self had insight to offer, including the correct name of the evasive, tip-of-my-tongue feeling that had been testing my patience. If a frustrating feeling like this has plagued you, too, whether it's naming an emotion or an old classmate, try a closet cleaning of your own and see what floats into your awareness.

## LET'S REVIEW

Well done, travelers. This was a hard stop on our journey, and you may be feeling emotionally drained or even physically tired (or both!). That's because excavating emotions and deconstructing feelings isn't an easy task, especially when we're grieving.

You've likely connected that all of our stops through this difficult stage of the process share the mind as a common denominator. I've presented them together in order to provide a framework for the rest of our expedition through the ambiguous grief process and, specifically, the next stage.

While no meditation or mindfulness practice is powerful enough to bring our loved ones back to us as they once were, or to undo the damage deployed by cognitive decline or TBI, we know that we can practice them for the benefit of our own minds. Doing so can ease the battle waging in the War Room between our ears and help to calm, collect, and even rewire not only what we think, but *how* we think. In this way, as we love ourselves with self-compassion and kindness, change begins to take place within us, and we begin to transform, to heal. With a commitment to understand, name, and confront our feelings, combined with "pre-acting" with our thoughts, we subtly begin to change and thereby relieve grief of its command post.

By gifting grand assumptions and becoming open to modalities we haven't been before, such as medication, therapy, meditation, and mindfulness, we become more aware of our outside world and can expand our ability to empathize. This doesn't mean you will suddenly feel like your old self again or that your loss will suddenly be "okay," but rather that you begin to see you have active choices in how you experience grief instead of passively waiting for time to heal your wound. One feeling at a time, one choice at a time, empowers you in healing over time. To help, you've just added the travel-ready tools of meditation and mindfulness for use anytime, anywhere. Remember that tools like therapy and medication are options to explore with your medical care team, too!

Maybe your activating event wasn't your parent's dementia diagnosis or a loved one's brain injury, but in being able to meet your own grief, and by doing ongoing work from the lessons in this chapter, you're likely better able to understand such stories and maybe even see parts of yourself in them. This is what I learned when I met My People—a group of ambiguous grievers who helped me to pinpoint the beguiling stage of grief that evaded me.

You'll meet them next, but before you continue, take whatever time you need to reflect. If your environment allows, now may be a good time to explore journaling. Simply collect your thoughts and connect to your heart by answering this question: "What does my head want to tell my heart?" Don't judge yourself; just write it out. If writing doesn't feel right to you, do what does feel good—draw, dance, or sing it out if you feel so called. If you'd rather not, that's okay, too—just take this time for a few deep breaths and hydrate.

Then, when you are ready, meet me at the next stop. There, you will find you will have a decision to make between two paths. While these roads may appear to be similar, they are alike only in name. I'm about to introduce you to both paths and share what has made all the difference for me between them, so pack your patience and treat yourself kindly as you travel on. Remember: for those moments when your thoughts are slippery and spiraling or the weight of your loss feels overwhelming, meditation and mindfulness provide an efficient, two-pronged counterattack. Get quiet, breathe, find your awareness, and remember that you are not the thoughts in your head.

## WISE WORDS ON EMOTIONS, MINDFULNESS, AND MEDITATION

"Fear is the path to the dark side. Fear leads to anger. Anger leads to hate. Hate leads to suffering."
—YODA, JEDI MASTER

"Feelings come and go like clouds in a windy sky. Conscious breathing is my anchor."
—THICH NHAT HANH, *STEPPING INTO FREEDOM: RULES OF MONASTIC PRACTICE FOR NOVICES*

"You better check yo' self before you wreck yo' self / cause I'm bad for your health / I come real stealth"
—ICE CUBE

"If you just sit and observe, you will see how restless your mind is. If you try to calm it, it only makes it worse, but over time it does calm, and when it does, there's room to hear more subtle things—that's when your intuition starts to blossom and you start to see things more clearly and be in the present more. Your mind just slows down, and you see a tremendous expanse in the moment. You see so much more than you could see before."
—STEVE JOBS

"Your vision will become clear only when you can look into your own heart. Who looks outside, dreams; who looks inside, awakes."
—CARL JUNG

## CHAPTER 3

# Hope, Personal Power, and the Women of Sex Monster Camp

"Where there is hope, there is life."
—ANNE FRANK

"I am not an optimist, but a great believer in hope."
—NELSON MANDELA

In the last chapter, we learned that grief is a response to loss, and the acute onset of intense emotions we experience in grieving is normal, largely universal, and as unique as the relationship we are grieving. In allowing these feelings, we can acquire tools to help us mourn in a healthy way, instead of resisting and adopting counterproductive or even harmful coping mechanisms. In taking responsibility for your own healing, you're acquiring tools to aid you in adapting to life with this loss. With a simple clerical tool you'll acquire in this chapter, I believe you will be better equipped to make an important and defining decision about your healing as well. Our first two stops have prepared us to tackle this one, and you'll be well able to see yourself through. This is the defining stage of the ambiguous grief process, so we'll spend a fair amount of time here—more than in any other place. Having spent ample time exploring this stop myself, I am excited to show you around.

What exactly makes the ambiguous griever's experience different? That one pesky feeling stage I could never isolate or identify by name but felt rotating in and out with the stages of grief is…drumroll…the experience of *hope*. Are you surprised? I was. To me, this discovery felt like a kind of betrayal. After all, we want hope, we need hope, and at times, hope was all I had. However, I soon found that hope wasn't what it seemed to be. As it turns out, it was this feeling stage that was commanding my whole experience of the stages of grief, and it was driving me in circles. Hope's co-conspirators (bargaining, anger, depression, etc.) had been taking turns at the wheel, and with no clear off-ramp, I was stuck on a perpetual roundabout of intense grief. Keep that in mind as we continue with a story about "My People," how I found them, and how meeting these resilient women in group therapy in the middle of the desert provided my first clues to exposing hope.

## SEX MONSTER CAMP

"I need to find My People," I wailed, sobbing into the phone. On the other end, my friend Steph was doing the best she could to provide comfort and offer suggestions, but being five hundred miles away, she had a limited ability to help. It was a few months post–Discovery Day, and my confusion was suffocating. "You're saying you want to go home for a while?" she asked. My answer was a quick, flat "No." That wasn't what I meant when I told her I needed My People, but I understood her confusion. Since I had moved from the Midwest, where I'd lived most of my life, to the South, where I knew no one, just three years earlier, Steph assumed I was crying out for the comfort of my friends and family back home. She wasn't exactly wrong—I missed them, and I needed them, of course. This evil blow would have been softened a bit, I think, had we not moved a twelve-hour drive from the life I knew. At least I would have had no less than a small legion of locals to help us through our dark days, where the daily duties of normal life weighed heavily: the endless carpools, middle and high school homework, soccer practices, meal prep, and twice-daily dog walking for our now bereft pup. But on this particular day, "My People" referred to the people like me, the betrayed and brokenhearted closet criers, privately grieving a loss they couldn't comprehend. I knew they had to be out there somewhere, also spinning, barely breathing from grief so deep they, too, were on the verge of losing themselves. I was desperate to understand how this had happened, and I was equally desperate to feel understood. I was caught between a desire to emotionally support my soon-to-be-ex and never wanting to see him again. I was working with Amy several times a week, but the pace of was moving slowly, and there was no manual to tell me whether I should focus my efforts in one direction or another.

I had started the overwhelming process of filing for divorce but didn't know what to do next. I knew that I needed to find others who could relate to my situation, having been through it themselves. The ones who had come out the other side and could hand over their manual, complete with itemized "dos and don'ts" and detailed notes in the margins. A manual of field notes from a veteran would surely grant me safe passage through the newly launched assault of grief and into healing.

"How do I help myself? I don't know what to do next. I don't know where to start," I pleaded to Steph through more tears.

"I want you to look up a place that helped me," she said once my sobbing slowed. "It's renowned for addiction treatment, but they are experts in other areas. I went twenty years ago after my brother's suicide. They are terrific in helping families impacted by trauma, and I'm sure they have something for you. They're located in Arizona, and there's always healing to be had when you're in the desert."

Steph was right; I called and learned that they did have something for me: a five-day group workshop called "Healing Intimate Treason." It was a hefty investment, but after a silent tally of all I'd discovered—dinner dates, gifts, and getaways—I quickly deemed the price tag, and myself, worthy and enrolled in their next available session.

*　　*　　*

Soon after arriving at The Meadows, I made my way to the small building marked with a red X on the map I had received at check-in. The building was perched atop a small mountain, separated from the main campus by a half mile of rocky terrain and a jagged row of cacti. Once a thriving cattle ranch, the center had repurposed the buildings for their outpatient clients after it bought the land a decade before. Looking up at it from below, I half expected to see tumbleweeds blow by. But as I neared the top, just mere steps from the building I was heading to, I gasped. The bluest of skies seemingly touched the roof of the little house in front of me. The hot air was soundless and still, not a breeze around me. The glorious expanse below stretched to meet the horizon in every direction. The Meadows offered up the first of many gifts—a rewarding view just for showing up. The tiny building had no entryway or foyer, so with one step through the front door, I was standing in the group space, which was no bigger than a college dorm room. Four women were already seated; only two seats were empty. I moved to the open seat in the center and instantly regretted it. Half a moment later, before I could change seats, a woman stepped inside and claimed the final seat beside the door. I envied her position closest to the door—it was the best one for a quick escape. We sat in silence, patiently waiting for our instructors to enter. A large, open-door cabinet stocked solely with boxes of tissues, too many to count, stood watch over our quiet semicircle. Scanning my fellow participants, I recognized the false calm each wore on her masked face, because I'd taken to wearing the same mask. Two more women, our facilitators (therapists? coaches? what were they anyway?), entered. They were both beautiful, and both offered a kind of parental confidence that brought ease to the room before anyone said a word. Smiling warmly at our group, one introduced herself as Nancy. She invited us to share our name, what brought us there, and what we hoped to get out of the retreat. After modeling what that would look like, her colleague, Elizabeth, introduced herself as well. I'd like to think that they asked who would like to go next or report that there was some gentle prodding to coax the first introduction, but that's not what happened. For some reason, a mere blink after Elizabeth finished, I was standing up and spilling my relief out onto the group.

"I'm Stephanie. I'm grieving the loss of my marriage, I just started the divorce process, and I'm here because I am desperate to meet all of you—My People." (I gestured with my arms opened wide.)

"Thank you, Stephanie, and thank you for being here. That was brave of you to go first," Nancy said. Then, nodding at me slowly: "You can sit down now." Suddenly I became aware that I was standing in front of the class, in between our two therapists—far from my chair. One by one, each woman introduced herself. Some weren't sure why they were there; they didn't want to believe they needed to be. One was so quiet when she spoke that Nancy had to ask her to start over three times. Another continued on, charging past the specific introductory format we were given and sharing shocking details none of us anticipated. Nancy tactfully and compassionately interrupted her in a way that showcased her experience doing so. Later in the week, we would learn that "oversharing" is a trauma response, but in the moment, this long-winded introduction made me feel better about the way I had done my own. After the introductions were finished, three things jumped out at me: (1) we were all betrayed and grieving; (2) these were, indeed, My People; and (3) everyone had stayed seated except me. (Ugh!)

Elizabeth handed us each a workbook, a guide that we would use throughout our time together. It had the look and even the smell of a new academic text, one that would help us understand our experience. Thumbing through the newly inked pages, I saw diagrams of the brain and how it works (or fails to), lists of new-to-me vocabulary words like "gaslighting" and "cognitive dissonance," and interactive pages for our own reflective writing answering questions like, "What were the signs you missed?" Our first session had begun.

Before breaking at midday, Nancy invited us to share more about ourselves. One by one, our motley crew spoke. An hour later, I felt more relief than I had in months. We were a cross-section of women: grandmothers, stepmothers, stay-at-home moms, retirees, executives, and returning workers. Some had come because they had made accidental discoveries like me, while others learned by confession, a keen-eyed co-worker, or an anonymous tipster. In the coveted chair beside the door sat Lucille, who had learned the devastating truth from her physician after her annual exam. After first denying she could have contracted a sexually transmitted disease from him, her husband eventually confessed and admitted to sleeping with hundreds of sex workers over most of their marriage. "All while seeing a therapist and lying to him, too!" she said, pounding her thigh with her tight, trembling fist. During that week, Lucille never used her seat by the door to escape, but none of us would have blamed her if she had.

Like Lucille, the rest of us—Maria, Patricia, Diane, Maya, and I—were angry, too.

Maya was the last to share her story. With her voice quiet and flat, most of us struggled to hear all of what she said about her handsome, successful husband, but all of us heard what she said at the end. "So," Maya concluded, "he's really mad right now. Saying that I'm making him out to be a monster. Saying I'm at 'Sex Monster Camp.'" Maybe it was the way soft-spoken Maya grew loud and imitated her husband's voice when she said it, or perhaps it was the absurdity of the name itself, but the room burst into laughter, Maya included. Someone quipped, "Sex Monster Camp! We need to make our own T-shirts!" and with that, my sisters of ambiguous grief had assembled, a shattered girl gang that ranged in age from thirty-seven to seventy-two years.

Though how we came to learn the truth of our activating event varied, what we learned had several common themes, among them our devastation. None of us had suspected a thing. Another commonality was that though we were united in betrayal trauma, no two of us had the same thoughts on our path forward. We were all still legally married, and all pursuing different actions: physical separation with joint finances, financial but not physical separation, divorce, annulment, and continuation of the marriage. We all determined that one wild card would be how our husbands behaved upon our return. But our leaders reminded us that we didn't need to decide anything in the moment and had several days ahead to get the information we needed to help us make the best choice for ourselves—whatever that may be.

Before that week, I struggled to articulate to a friend how the nuances of betrayal trauma and my unknown grief were impacting me. "It's one pain to lose the future you thought you had in front of you," I explained, "but it is another pain entirely to lose the past you thought you had lived, and on top of it all, I don't hate him. I miss him." My friend had nodded, as if saying, "I understand you." But her face belied a confusion that told me she didn't. How could she, I supposed. Normal people in healthy relationships have no need to question whether their pasts were authentic or not. But when I shared that same sentiment with My People, all heads nodded in agreement. Not only did they understand, but, finally, I felt understood.

Though I found My People through a group therapy intensive, there are other ways to find yours. Check online for web-based or in-person support groups within your community.

You may need to try a few before you find the best fit—that's normal. Getting clear about what you want in a group before you begin will help! For example, accountability, community, encouragement, fellowship, etc. To help get you started, I've also included additional resources in the back of the book.

## My People, My Mirror

As we shared more each day, I found a small comfort in learning that I wasn't the only one who had been conflicted about antidepressants or was finding relief through meditation. Though our stories were different, all of us were eager to feel better, to be freed from the prisons of our own minds, where until now we had been held in solitary confinement, left alone with thoughts we simply couldn't make sense of. We were desperate in part because we craved validation for our pasts and desired to find some meaning within the mirage of our marriages. Like the women around me, I had spent countless hours parsing through years of memories, not knowing what parts of my relationship had been real. Earnestly, my mind had been working to make sense of things and scurried to cut and paste together a narrative from the varied scripts of my life over the past twenty years. I would dig through photos, looking for a noticeable difference I'd missed in real time, or replay conversations in my head, connecting dots of contradictions—a daily game for anyone trying to reconcile a betrayal. I despised playing it, but I couldn't stop, even though I longed to. It was clear that My People had been locked in the same mental game, and it was the excruciating inability to integrate our newly discovered truths that was the source of our communal desperation.

Throughout that week we sat in our semicircle in the old rancher's cottage at the top of the hill. Our facilitators masterfully guided our conversations, highlighting and informing along the way. They gave lessons on human psychology—basic stuff that I had once learned but had long forgotten, like common stress reactions to grief and techniques for managing emotional triggers. Others consisted of understanding how the brain works and why certain behaviors and coping mechanisms might begin. We hit padded blocks with padded bats and expressed our grief on paper and in voice. We reviewed our own histories and relational patterns, and we released our anger in tear-filled ceremonies, supporting one another silently, as each read from an itemized list of heartbreak. By our final day, we had come to understand that we could not change the past, and we could not predict the future, but we could choose how we responded to our grief, our trauma, and the new lives we were charting for ourselves. Every single one of the tissues in the wall of boxes had been used. Each of us holding our last tissue box, we left the small rancher's cottage and gathered in seats around a fire pit outside. There, Nancy and Elizabeth guided us through our final release, and soon we were all sobbing, taking turns proclaiming each unique pain one tissue at a time. The tissues caught our sacred tears until we had none left to offer. We sat together in silence, exhausted and empowered as we watched our leaders slowly shovel the pile of tear tissues into the kiln, where they burned to ash. We said goodbye, and with promises to stay connected, each left the desert and headed for home.

## At-Home Group Therapy

Upon returning to our respective lives, My People stayed in contact with scheduled phone calls and an ongoing text loop. Though we were spread throughout four time zones, our fellowship continued to grow, and over the seasons, our bond strengthened. On our first conference call, Diane shared an update on herself and her marriage. Though she was still unsure what she was going to do, for the time being, she had insisted on physical separation. Living apart provided her with the physical and emotional space she needed to focus on and care for herself. She shared, "I have a lot to reconcile, not only about my marriage, but about myself. By living alone, I'm able to pay better attention to me; my thoughts, my feelings, and my desires." From what she told us, it sounded as though her husband was using this time to focus on himself, too. We knew he had his own People: a group of men who had acted similarly in their marriages and with whom he attended group therapy several times a week. He had wanted the same for her, which is in part why she came to the desert. But now he was asking if they could begin couples' counseling. In addition to his individual therapy appointments, she shared that his therapy-laden schedule was his choice and made him accountable in one form or another, every day of the week. Though not much was made of Diane's update in the moment, it proved an additive data point for us all, and one that inspired much discussion later.

As our weekly calls continued, My People became my at-home, unsupervised group therapy; it wasn't the most ideal, but it was what we needed, so we made it work. During this time, we updated one another with new developments and shared insights and other resources. We never judged or condemned, but rather we listened and supported by simply witnessing one another. Our group acted as mirrors for one another, each of us receiving and reflecting images of behavior that was sometimes hard to see. For me, such honest reflection proved critically important, when, on the one-year anniversary of my activating event, the floor fell out from under me again, this time in the form of forgotten fragments of that day.

These memories were constructed like segments of the nightly news, where I was "live on the scene" serving as both subject and reporter with fresh, developing details from the morning in question. I got busy examining each memory like the hopeful new clue that it was. Perhaps one was the missing piece that I needed to make sense of it all. But when I relayed my exciting news to My People on our weekly phone call, Patricia set me straight. Wise from doing her own work toward healing, she gently reminded me that anniversary dates can trigger such memories—but I didn't see it that way and dismissed her when she cautioned me about slipping back into old thinking patterns. I respected her, but I didn't agree and decided to save my theories for my next session with Amy, six days away. I knew Amy would not only "get it," but suspected she'd likely be pretty proud of me for wanting to dig in, too.

In the meantime, the highlight reel continued playing in my dreams, and I grew exponentially more agitated during the day. The memories became more vivid and wouldn't go away, unfazed by my counterattack of medication, meditation, and intention setting. When I finally met with Amy and shared what was happening, she didn't respond as I had imagined. Not only did she double-cross me by siding with Patricia, she challenged me by asking why I thought uncovering more painful details would help me heal. Before I could bounce back from my surprise, she delivered another blow.

Amy explained that I was experiencing the surfacing of repressed memories, a common occurrence for those who experience a traumatic event—and yes, frequently triggered by experiences like anniversaries, sounds, or even fragrances. While it's not wrong to face these memories, she said, it's important to understand the intention behind them. To try to dredge up potentially damaging memories for the sake of having more information wasn't prudent. However, done another way, it could be. After talking it through with me, she recommended that I begin sessions of eye movement desensitization and reprocessing (EMDR) therapy, an interactive and intense therapeutic technique that targets memories "stuck" in the amygdala, the part of the brain controlling fight or flight. "EMDR essentially frees memories so that that they can be processed and integrated by the rest of the brain," Amy explained. I nodded my enthusiasm. "It's not for everyone, and while I believe it could help you, I want you to hear me, Steph: it's tough, draining work."

Good ole Amy, Chief of the Fun Police.

Though I hadn't initially agreed with the insight Patricia offered me, I soon found that the truth was that I rejected it because I didn't want it to be true. Not only had she been right about the reason for my newfound memories, but after two months of weekly EMDR therapy, I found that Amy had been right on both counts: EMDR was tough, draining work, and it did help me. Though the weekly process of surfacing those submerged memories was a ruthless act, it allowed me to purposefully examine each one and begin the painstaking task of safely processing them. EMDR didn't erase or remove those memories, but it allowed me to view them objectively, like a third-party observer, aware and empathizing but unattached from the first-person experience of it all. I was now simply watching the highlight reel, not starring in the lead role. In that way I was able to "file" the reel accordingly and observe it from a safe distance, where it could no longer harm me. Being able to view my experience in this way was transformative; not only did this therapy form a "sort and file" on my nervous system and those trauma-induced memories, it turned my grief down a notch, too. It was still there, but with less intensity; it was as though my grief had put down the bullhorn and was now using its inside voice. With those memories now safely stored, I began to wonder if there was room for new ones.

## HELLO, HOPE

Twelve months after we first met in the rancher's cottage on top of the hill, the women of Sex Monster Camp traveled back to the desert to reunite for a relaxing long weekend. Within hours, the name for that feeling came to me. I heard my soul self loud and clear and knew the message was true: it was hope. It had been hope all along. In addition to anger, denial, bargaining, depression, and acceptance, each of us had expressed or demonstrated that she was also experiencing hope as a substantial part of her grief—but not in a good way.

Because it was expressed differently for each of us, I didn't initially see that it was actually originating from the same place. But like siblings born of the same parents who look and act nothing alike, so had we all birthed hope, but each of us dressed it differently. We dressed our hope like a paper doll, mixing and matching accessories, with an infinite number of combinations, in search of our best look. No combination felt quite right, but instead of acknowledging that, we'd start over again thinking that the correct combination was in front of us, so we kept working while our hope grew torn and tattered. We were a group of hope-filled contradictions driven by conflicting emotions and strong feelings about our loved one, our situation, and ourselves. For some, our hope was outfitted in anxious fear, martyrdom, or aggressive anger. For others, our hope wore pretty ideas and comforting thoughts. For all of us, hope was at the very core of what we had been talking about: we hoped to reconcile with our husbands; hoped they would marry a floozy who would cheat on them; hoped our children would never know the truth; hoped our children would learn the truth; hoped to reinvent ourselves and build a new life; hoped to hold on as long as we could; hoped to never see our husbands again; hoped they would change and come back to us; even hoped for their death so we could fully grieve our loss with wakes, witnesses, and casseroles, like normal widows.

Our hope went on and on. Yours may, too.

---

### Exercise 11 | How Do You Hope?

Think about the loss of your loved one. What do you hope for? Write out as many hopes as come to your mind in the next five minutes. Don't judge or censor yourself. Get quiet and pour your hope out here. Then take a break if you need to and continue on when you're ready. We'll come back to your list later.

I hope…

---

## Hope in Ambiguous Grief

With help from others sharing their ambiguous grief stories as well as my continued conversations with My People, I began sharing my idea of hope as an experience in ambiguous grief.

I shared the idea with a handful of trusted people, including Amy and Dr. Sophia Caudle, the psychologist I had seen for EMDR. Since we were no longer working together as therapist and patient, we met to discuss my hypothesis on hope and decided to team up and explore this idea. Creating an assessment tool as well as a survey with over four hundred respondents, we discovered some interesting results about ambiguous grief and the process toward healing, which informed the Ambiguous Grief Process Model.

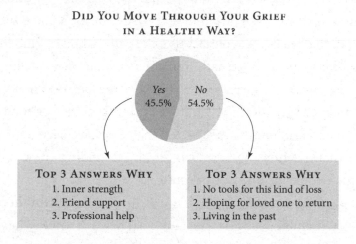

DID YOU MOVE THROUGH YOUR GRIEF
IN A HEALTHY WAY?

Yes
45.5%

No
54.5%

TOP 3 ANSWERS WHY
1. Inner strength
2. Friend support
3. Professional help

TOP 3 ANSWERS WHY
1. No tools for this kind of loss
2. Hoping for loved one to return
3. Living in the past

We found that hope presented for people experiencing ambiguous grief in two different ways: **internally** (with a focus on self) and **externally** (with a focus on the lost relationship). In addition, we found ambiguous grievers cycled in and out of both, all with unique intervals and no defined timeframe. I was struck by the answers given for why or why not respondents felt they had moved or were moving through their grief in a healthy way. The most common answer indicated those who were not moving through in a healthy way felt this was the case because they lacked the tools to do so. This insight helped to shape my own understanding of grief on a macro level, and it affirmed just how little we talk about loss, bereavement, grief, and mourning. We are more connected to our outside world than ever before, yet so many of us are suffering in our inner worlds, isolated and unable to navigate through a grief that goes largely ignored by others and sometimes even by ourselves. We live in abundance with modern devices that connect us externally, while lacking the ability to connect internally and construct our own healing.

Perhaps most surprising to me about the nature of hope in ambiguous grief was the duration of time spent experiencing each and just how many reported that they have been hoping for their relationship to return for an astounding amount of time—some for a decade or more.

Seeking to understand more fully how and why hope impacts ambiguous grievers, and what helps or hinders healing, I began following my curiosities and independently pursued the topic. Culled from many sources—from interviews with clinicians and authors to insights from others experiencing ambiguous grief—this is by no means an exhaustive study, but what I found and found to be missing helped me to understand the nuances of hope in a new way.

## The Hope Survey

In my hope-specific survey, I define hope as a feeling of expectation, longing, or desire for the relationship to return to its previous state. The answers revealed an untold narrative about hope: though it's planted abundantly, it is generally fruitless. Of the two hundred respondents who indicated they had experienced hope:

- 56% citied external hope behaviors ranging from "several times a day" to "several times a month."
- 41% indicated that their external hope behaviors were now "rarely to never."
- 94% shared that their relationship has not returned to its previous state.

### How Long?
*Length of time experiencing external hope*

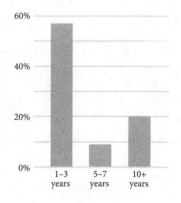

**AGP Survey**
Of over the 400 people surveyed, 94% reported they have grieved or are currently grieving the loss of a loved one still living

**Two Hopes**
57% reported more external hope
13% reported more internal hope
30% showed cycling between the two

Unfortunately, this doesn't necessarily mean that 6 percent of relationships *do* return; while a small number are reconciled or renewed, the vast majority are not. This 6 percent is because of other variables reported, namely the physical death of their loved one. Understanding this, we can rule out external hope as effective toward restoration. You probably see that what remains is to accept that your relationship will (most likely to highly probably) not return as it once was, which makes the path of internal hope your best option to healing. If you are not excited about that option, I understand. I wasn't at first either—and if it were simple, we'd all be doing it, right?

It's not that simple because hope is also confusing, especially since we grow up with universal ideals of hope as affirmative. But hope, like love, is complicated. A great many people have painted a picture of hope as being universally positive, almost heroic; after all, hope is a virtue that sustains the brokenhearted, motivates the beleaguered, and inspires action. Hope feels good, and I believe that we need hope to endure our unpredictable human experience; but I also believe there's an important caveat to consider. By analyzing survey responses, loving My People through their losses, managing myself through my own, and interviewing other ambiguous grievers, I discovered something else surprising about hope in ambiguous grief: **when hope is misdirected, it is as dangerous as it is good.**

If you're feeling like I've insulted your mother right now, you're not alone. You may be feeling like hope for your loved one is all you have left. I know how that feels, because I felt the same way. What I've found is that the more we understand what hope looks like and how it shows up through the process of ambiguous grief, the sooner we can determine which hope we're dealing with when it presents. If we deconstruct hope by applying Plutchik's theory (see page 39), then I see hope as a feeling state created by combining anticipation + optimism + relief. Sign me up, right?! Not so fast, and here's why: since hope presents in two different ways for ambiguous grievers, the hope that is driving determines the destination. Let's take a closer look.

## THE TWO ROADS OF HOPE

Internal hope and external hope each have their own road, and both will move you off the roundabout of intense grief feelings. The roads are similar only in name; the experience of each, as well as its final destination, is decidedly different. One leads to recovery, and another to a form of grief known as prolonged grief disorder (formerly known as complicated grief, but more on that later). Think of it this way: hope is a double agent working for both sides. Sometimes hope shows up with instructions that drive your healing, and at other times hope carries out orders that keep you on the roundabout of grief. Once you are able to identify which hope you're dealing with, you can also decide what to do with it.

Because the nature of grief is ambiguous and amorphous,

with no predictable shape helping to structure a schedule of activities, it's most likely that you will cycle back and forth between the two hopes before advancing closer to your ultimate destination. Cycling may look like confused feelings, blurred intentions, bids for familiarity, or proudly making gains only to be drawn backward and discouraged again. This is normal and nothing to feel badly about. In fact, an emerging model of grief, known as the Dual Process Model, maintains that a helpful component to coping with bereavement is taking breaks from your grief. (It is exhausting, isn't it?)

Similarly, as ambiguous grievers shift in and out of both hopes, it's helpful to notice when you are cycling so that you can reroute yourself, or at the very least decide what you want to do. In my survey, data revealed 30 percent of respondents were engaged in cycling, myself included. Thanks to witnessing My People, I could clearly see how all of us had been cycling the entire time, in and out of hope for both our old lives and our new. But, as time went on and I became more aware of my feelings, thoughts, and actions, cycling became increasingly less frequent. Over time, I became astute at identifying which road I was traveling and "locating" myself on my homemade ambiguous grief map. This became critical for me later, and will for you, too, once it becomes time to make a decision. Just as we did at the start of our journey, we have to assess where we are along the way in order to orient ourselves in the direction we wish to go. With that in mind, let's explore this stop more thoroughly with the intention of determining your current location on the map of ambiguous grief. You can do that by learning about each of these routes, their peaks and pitfalls, and where they lead. As you do, take note of your thoughts, emotions, questions, and revelations. First up is the path of external hope, a familiar road that starts out easy, but doesn't stay that way for long.

## Examining External Hope

External hope is a feel-good path. At least in the beginning. This path keeps us focused on our loved one and in the primary position of holding vigil. This path longs for the past relationship to return as it once was or hopes the person lost to us will change back to who they used to be or who we thought they were. In this way, this path allows us to stay connected to our loved one: those with external hope often spend their time and energy consumed with activities that look like finding help for or pledging loyalty to their loved one. This may include researching new treatment options to help their loved one, obsessively seeking alternative therapies for their loved one, negotiating with the loved one on behavior modifications, working to reconnect the loved one to old friends or social structures, fixating on their loved one's whereabouts, or trying to be a part of their loved one's activities. Bids for familiarity are also present, whereby the person seeks to reconnect with their loved one or attempts to engage them with shared memories or past shared experiences. While "hey, remember when..." may not be a bid for familiarity for a caregiver attempting to jostle the memory of their loved one with a brain injury, it is for relationships that have been more intentionally severed. My People helped me identify "remember when" messages as bids that are rooted in external hope.

By staying focused on your loved one, whether by being attentive to their needs, or via components from your lost relationship, travelers on this path are writing their own hall pass out of an honest examination of their pain. This is understandable, since it is far less painful to stay focused externally, even if it's a false attachment, than to confront an agonizing reality and the finality of letting go. Grievers in external hope may say things like:

"Even though the relationship I love is no longer as it once was...

"I will never give up on them."
"I will wait for them to get clean and sober."
"I will focus on a cure for their disease."
"It's my job or duty to fix this."
"I will never leave them."

### Inspecting Internal Hope

Contrary to the comfort felt at the start of external hope, internal hope feels more like a steep climb from start to finish, often in the dark. That's because internal hope is largely uncharted territory. While you may have ventured in on occasion, it's likely you stayed as long as you could but eventually turned back to a more familiar path. All of which is understandable, and all of which I did, too. It can be challenging because **internal hope is directed to the self in the present, with attention to our life as it is, not as we wish it to be**. This hope accepts that the relationship cannot be restored as it once was and focuses on reimagining a future in which it's possible to thrive without the loved one or reestablishing the relationship back into the ambiguous griever's life. Initially, this hope feels excruciatingly painful, and as a result it requires a motivated mindset. This is because in order to "succeed" at internal hope, you have to decline the feel-good temptation of the other options and focus efforts only on yourself—even when you know you could get a reprieve by turning back.

Remember Diane's update to our group earlier in this chapter? Though it wasn't obvious at the time, both she and her husband were largely modeling behaviors aligned with internal hope. Though Diane wasn't sure if she would stay married, upon returning home from the desert, she had taken action to focus on herself with physical separation. From there, she built a personalized regimen of internal hope with daily prayer, weekly individual therapy, and intentional time dedicated to some of her favorite things: soothing cups of tea, planting and tending to her garden, revisiting favorite poems, and discovering new ones. Eventually, she turned attention to her marriage and accepted her husband's invitation to begin couples' counseling, where they both shared new insights and understandings of their healing. For over three years, each maintained the practice of internal hope; focusing on their own healing and accepting their current reality without attempts to manage the other toward a desired outcome. For Diane, it took this long to confidently determine a decision about her marriage. The eventual outcome and the time it takes to get there are different for everyone, so try not focus on the time that is passing and instead stay focused on the work you are doing in the present. A good way to do this is to identify your own behaviors and, like Diane, commit to caring for yourself as best you can.

Those in internal hope often spend their time and energy on activities that look like self-care, with a focus on themselves as a person *without* their loved one. This may include increased attention to their physical being through exercise or appearance; exploring new activities that bring joy, excitement, peace, or fulfillment to themselves; connecting to new social, religious, or spiritual groups; planning their own celebratory events (a birthday party, milestone trip, etc.); or any activities that promote their overall well-being. Those in internal hope may say:

"Even though the relationship I love is no longer as it once was...:

"I will focus on myself."
"I will be present in each moment."

"I will create a life I love."

"I will be open to meeting new people and trying new things."

"I will get through this and grow as I go."

## Cycling

Since these two different kinds of hope aren't mutually exclusive and can be experienced simultaneously, remember that spending time in and out of both is natural. Especially since one feels much better than the other, it's not unusual to gain ground on the prickly path of internal hope only to suddenly abandon your route, seeking refuge on the less painful path of external hope. This is because external hope is comfortable, especially for those with tendencies toward codependency (the excessive emotional or psychological reliance on a partner, typically one who requires support). Think of cycling shaped like the number 8 and serving as a kind of highway bypass system seamlessly connecting the two paths of hope. In this "8" shape, internal hope is on top and external hope is below, and the convergence point in between is filled with those who have not yet decided, or aren't aware they're even there!

Directing our energy and focus to our loved one in return for feeling a certain way or maintaining a personal narrative isn't a healthy coping mechanism in grief, or ever in life, really. Instead, though it may take more time to adjust to the practice of internal hope, it will become less arduous the more you do so. That isn't to say you will find it an easy trek; it's not, but it is one that introduces more joy and moves you in the direction of recovery. Although one hope is more prevalent than the other at any given time, both hopes "live" in a person. It's easy to identify the travelers who spend a significant amount of time cycling through both hopes because they are conflicted. With their heart and mind at war and neither allowing the other to advance too far ahead, it's difficult to gain ground in either direction. You can look for clues of cycling by paying attention to your own thoughts and actions. You may declare your decision to erect firm boundaries one day, only to deconstruct them days later. You may appear at odds with yourself or your loved ones, and your energy may oscillate between frenetic and depressed. Above all, sustained cycling is signaled with mental, physical, and emotional exhaustion—the toll paid for too much time on this precarious path.

## Plotting Your Coordinates

With that insight, think about where you are on the map. Are you identifying more with behaviors and feelings that describe internal or external hope? Maybe it's a comfortable cadence cycling in and out of both, or perhaps in cycling you are driving in circles, riding the peaks and valleys of both roads of hope in a never-ending crazy-eight pattern, all while making yourself dizzy in the process. Let's use the next exercise to pinpoint your present location.

## Exercise 12 | Location Services On

Are you in external hope, internal hope, or cycling between both? Return to the "How Do You Hope" exercise (page 96) and review your hopes. Read each one carefully and assign an "I" if it indicates hope for yourself or an "E" if your hope indicates focus on your loved one. Add up how many "I"s and "E"s you have and write them below.

Write your scores here: Internal hope _____

External hope _____

The hope with the higher number is currently driving your healing. Numbers that are equal or close in range by a point or two indicate you are likely cycling in between the two.

Now, complete this sentence by indicating where you are with hope.

On the ambiguous grief map, I am currently:

_____ .

Remember, you are collecting information, and there is no right or wrong answer. You are taking an honest look at where you are so that you can decide where you want to go. Without honestly knowing where you are now, you can't plot your path forward. Now that you know where you are, the next step is to assess the options ahead of you before continuing on. Take a break, and when you're ready, I'll provide an overview of three different options and details about their final destinations so you can decide where you want to head next.

## THREE OPTIONS, TWO PATHS,
## ONE DECISION

You have identified where you are, and with that knowledge you now have a decision to make. I apologize in advance—this may not be easy. But thanks again to the Ancient Greeks, I have a helpful tool to share. Certainly, this isn't the first difficult decision you've had to make, and you aren't the first to be faced with one. We know that tough choices have been plaguing humans for millennia, and just as the Ancient Greeks examined emotions, so too they looked at decisions. The topic can be traced to AD 125, when it appeared in a compilation based on the teachings of the Stoic philosopher Epictetus titled the *Enchiridion.*[1] This title translates as the "book at hand," or, as we say today, "handbook," and the book has been interpreted and adapted in texts, scripture, and lectures around the world for over two thousand years. This handbook offers fifty-three practical principles advising readers on how to live a peaceful, moral life and how to find contentment in all experiences. The first principle anchors Stoic teachings with a message about personal power—one that, when adapted by ambiguous grievers, becomes a tool for healing.

**The first principle:** "There are things which are within our power, and there are things which are beyond our power. Within our power are opinion, aim, desire, aversion, and, in one word, whatever affairs are our own. Beyond our power are body, property, reputation, office, and, in one word, whatever are not properly our own affairs."

To paraphrase: at all times, determine what is within your control and what is not.

**The second principle:** further, Epictetus cautions that there are emotional consequences in our choices—both in trying to control what is outside of us, and in accepting that which is beyond our power. He wrote, "You must not allow yourself any inclination, however slight, toward the attainment of the others; but that you must entirely quit some of them, and for the present postpone the rest. But if you would have these, and possess power and wealth likewise, you may miss the latter in seeking the former; and you will certainly fail of that by which alone happiness and freedom are procured."

**The third principle:** Epictetus assesses that all unpleasing human experiences can be viewed through this lens, but to benefit from the practice, we must also be able to execute the final piece, which is to accept and detach from that which we cannot control. "Examine it by those rules which you have," he writes, "and first and chiefly, by this: whether it concerns the things which are within our own power, or those which are not; and if it concerns anything beyond our power, be prepared to say that it is nothing to you."

Epictetus promoted the principles of Stoic philosophy as so important that they should be kept "ready at hand." His intent was for these principles to become ingrained in our consciousness and therefore accessible whenever we need them.

Today, we know Epictetus as a respected philosopher, but I think it's worth contemplating why that is. I suspect it is, in part, because his teachings posit action and offer insights that improve a difficult part of our immutable human condition: suffering. His personal experience of suffering—he was born into slavery and often abused—surely shaped his perspective and allowed him to confirm his own tested theories. But remember, he wasn't a privileged pupil or a member of an influential family, either of which would have promoted his cause. Epictetus was credentialed in an even more important way: he was a slave who learned how to ease his suffering, and that made him an experiential expert. He wasn't hearing about enduring such pain from second- or third-hand accounts, he had survived it himself. I believe this perspective translates to his teachings and is why they resonated then and remain relevant today—and is why these teachings helped me confront reality and step into my personal power.

---

### Exercise 13 | Sort and File

Return again to your list of hopes. Sort each of the hopes that you listed into one of two "files." Channel your inner Stoic, face reality, and file accordingly. Which of your hopes are in your power and which are beyond your power?

Hopes that are within my power:

Hopes that are beyond my power:

Facing our reality can be painful, but it is also a sobering act that gifts us with clarity. You have just identified what is and isn't in your control; what you do with that information is up to you.

---

## THE PATH TO TRAVEL

Armed with the clarity of what is within our power and what is beyond our power, imagine that we are now at an intersection with a decision to make. Whether you feel confident of your choice or aren't remotely close to a decision, let's take the Stoic's approach and review the options of each path, with attention to the consequences and final destinations of each. In doing so, you can affirm your choice or gain clarity.

### Option 1: External Hope

Our first option is external hope. We know that when an ambiguous griever prolongs their focus on their loved one instead of themselves, the cycling in and out of internal hope diminishes. With less self-focus and their internal hope reserves depleted, their focus is set outside of themselves and onto their loved one. Of course, it's normal to focus efforts on helping our loved ones, but how long and to what extent we do so merits monitoring. We know that bereavement is universal and that we respond to our bereavement with grief. Most people can begin to reorient themselves to life post-loss.

But not everyone is able to do so, which makes the consequences of traveling this road important to understand.

### External Hope Risks and Consequences:
### The Potential of Prolonged Grief Disorder

For those of us who demonstrate the signs of acute grief twelve months after loss, or who display a disproportionate response (by whatever our cultural or religious norms would measure), something other than external hope or cycling may be happening. It may be prolonged grief disorder (PGD), which up until 2020 was known as "complicated grief." Recognized by the World Health Organization as a diagnosable condition in 2018 and by the American Psychiatric Association in 2020, PGD is the occurrence of a persistent and pervasive grief response characterized by persistent longing or yearning and/or preoccupation accompanied by at least three of eight additional symptoms: disbelief; intense emotional pain; feelings of identity confusion; avoidance of reminders of the loss; feelings of numbness, intense loneliness, or meaninglessness; and difficulty engaging in ongoing life. This is an important understanding for ambiguous grievers because lingering in external hope for too long may make us vulnerable to PGD.

In PGD, the bereaved are emotionally "stuck" and seemingly unable to adapt to grief in a healthy way. They may struggle to understand what is causing their pain or feel unable to separate themselves from their loss. Their loss may come to define their identity and seem to be all they want to talk about, or, conversely, they may have difficulty accepting the loss and be unable to talk about it at all. They may perceive their life to be behind them, with a hopeless future ahead.

If that felt heavy to read, imagine what it must be like to live in this space. With compassion, I make the grand assumption that no person knowingly chooses to slide into this quicksand-like state. Holding that as true, I think it's important we tread lightly for those grief companions among us wading into this water. They may not know that they are or know how to climb out. Through education and understanding, perhaps we can help one another know the signs of PGD, remembering that it's not specific to ambiguous grief, but all grieving. Those who are experiencing prolonged grief disorder may say things like:

> "I'm not sure what happened; I keep thinking about what I could have done differently."
> "I'm keeping their favorite groceries stocked and a place set at the table for them."
> "I can't think about anything else."
> "I don't feel like anyone understands why I'm still struggling."
> "My pain is just as raw as when it first happened."

If you recognize that you or a loved one are making similar comments, remember that being aware of PGD doesn't qualify you as an Armchair Amy, so be careful not to diagnose yourself or diagnose others. Instead, if you think you may be experiencing PGD or are at risk for it, be sure to talk to a qualified therapist. Be mindful of some of the associated risk factors: prior history of a mood disorder or anxiety disorder; loss of a partner or child; or a loss that is sudden, unexpected, or violent. Remember that all grief experiences are unique to the person and to the lost relationship.

## Option 2: Internal Hope

Our second option is internal hope. We know that this hope is self-focused and practiced only after the person experiencing grief has begun to accept the reality of their loss. Remember that this doesn't mean our grief is "gone" or that we don't wish it could be different, but rather that we are able to recognize it is not within our power to make it different. Those practicing internal hope coexist with their grief in a healthier manner, understanding that it is a normal response to loss. For those who are able to withstand and process the many, often conflicting feelings surrounding their loss, they know that discomfort is temporary. Unlike external hope, this path is most painful at the beginning but eases in approach of the final destination.

## Risks and Consequences

Just as with any decision, there are consequences to embracing the path of internal hope. Bluntly, the initial cost of this choice is additional, layered emotional upheaval. This may feel overwhelming and can be acutely painful, because we are detaching from a person we love, possibly to whom we feel inextricably linked. It may feel as though we are severing our own limb to escape from a trap, but, while brutally painful, the consequence of this choice is that we survive.

This path will likely require additional healing tools and a commitment to strengthening your resilience, so, for some, this choice becomes more daunting and may appear insurmountable. I suspect, though, that the biggest inherent risk we take by choosing internal healing is accountability. Not to the loved one we are grieving, or to our family and friends whose opinions may matter, but to ourselves. When we take personal accountability for our own healing, some scary questions may arise that could dissuade some from committing to this path.

For me, those questions were:

"What if I choose this path only to find that it's too hard?"

"What if I choose this path only to find more misery?"

"What if I commit to go on and live a revised life, but I fail?"

"What if I commit to this path, but can't find joy again?"

"What if I never get to recovery?"

I get it. To choose this path is to own our story and make ourselves accountable to the outcome. To choose this path is to choose to focus on what is within our power, and that can feel very scary, especially because we have to let go of someone we love to get there. But for those enduring this path, the payoff is rich. Internal hope is the only choice that leads to recovery, a space where we are healthfully coexisting with our grief and honoring our pain, our loss, and our journey. Not everyone who commits to the internal hope path will discover recovery, but there is no way to recovery without traveling the path of internal hope.

## CHOOSE YOUR OWN PATH

Now that you understand the two hopes and have your power files in order, one question remains: what hope do you choose now? I invite you to search your heart, think thoughtfully about this question, and answer once you know. If you still aren't sure, examine your notes from the exercises in this book for clues and remember that there is no judgment. Sort yourself into one of the two groups outlined below and follow the instructions for the path you've selected.

### Group 1: The Path of Internal Hope

If you choose to continue on the path of internal hope, take a break, grab some water, and treat yourself to a five-minute meditation. When you are ready, meet me on the next page.

## Group 2: The Path of External Hope

If you choose to continue on the path of external hope, our time together ends here, at least for now. That doesn't mean I don't understand your decision—I do. Letting go is hard, and for some, myself included, it's equally as painful as the initial loss itself. As much as I want you to move on with me, your choice is yours to make. I can neither will your effort nor carry you out of your grief; only you can do that. Until you are ready, remember to use the tools you have acquired thus far and know you have an open invitation to rejoin the journey whenever you choose. When you're ready to start down the path of internal hope—which I encourage you to do—I'll have some tools to share that may aid in the agony of letting go.

## Group 3: Cycling

If you aren't ready to commit to one or the other and feel you need to stay in cycling, I invite you to take time to reflect and process your thoughts and feelings about this. As you do, seek to understand exactly why you're wanting this option. Perhaps cycling in and out of both hopes feels comfortable for you because you've been doing it for so long, and, though you may not like it, at least you know what to expect. Maybe cycling is a reprieve from grief and allows you to feel something else for a while. Or, maybe you're like Maya and me—both of us talked a big game about focusing on ourselves, but experienced countless false starts on the road to our "new life." Inevitably, whenever either of us spent too much time walking that "new life" path of internal hope, we'd become tormented with guilt and overwhelmed with sorrow at the mere thought of moving on, feeling as if in doing so, we were abandoning a deeply loved part of ourselves. Keep in mind that you can, and likely will, continue to cycle. There is no time constraint on your cycling, and, since you are grieving at your pace, it's okay to cycle at your own pace, too. It's possible that you may always default to this space, cycling in and out of your grief for the rest of your life. It's also possible that you can move forward in healing and toward recovery while still cycling—although it's a slow-motion dance of two steps forward, one step back, you can still ambiguous-grief-cha-cha yourself to recovery. Just like naming our feelings makes them easier to experience, proclaiming your desired destination will serve you the same way. No matter how far away the joy and happiness of recovery feel today, proclaiming your desire to get there will act as a trail marker as you make your way, which will help you reorient as you cycle. I understand if you're not ready to firmly commit to the path of internal hope, but if you are willing to proclaim recovery as your desired destination, then I hope you'll join me. Consider it a trial run, and you won't be alone—I'm just about to start the next leg of the journey. Setting our sights toward recovery, let's keep reading!

## BOUND FOR RECOVERY, BUT FIRST: ACCOUNTABILITY

You're now carrying the same tools I held when I made the decision to exit the roundabout and set a course toward recovery. We are together in this, so this concept is important—getting comfortable asking for and accepting support is paramount. It's much harder to climb this mountain alone, and it's also not necessary.

Keep in mind that you are building a new habit, which can be hard, especially in the beginning. According to a 2018 study published by the *British Journal of General Practice*, it takes about ten weeks for a new habit to form.[2] With this in mind, it's key to use your tools to help you stay the course. Consistent accountability to Your People can be helpful here. Not only can they support and encourage you as you work on internal hope, they can also point out when you are cycling or, worse, sliding down the path of external hope and possibly into the quicksand that is PGD.

But like those marathons I once referenced to Amy, understand that this endeavor can only be achieved by your own fortitude. You don't have to be a runner to know that reading books on how to run a marathon won't get you across the finish line—you have to actually train by running. Experiencing internal hope in ambiguous grief is like that, too. You can expect it will test you, but if you make the commitment, summon your strength, and train yourself in increments, you can get to the finish line. Yes, it's focused, intentional work, but speaking as someone who made it through: it's time and effort well spent.

## Where Do We Go from Here?

Even if you know that internal hope is the right choice for you, be prepared for the possibility of running into unforeseen sadness, too. Though it may feel exciting to make the decision of committing to internal hope, that also means you are deciding to move out of external hope, an experience you've come to know. That part of your grief has been an intimate part of your being, perhaps for some time, but that doesn't mean it's been good for your well-being. Through the exercises in this chapter, you may have discovered that your acts of external hope are the only things remaining that keep you feeling connected to your old relationship. Even more, your acts of external hope may be the last point of access to who you once were in your relationship. For instance, for me, I was a wife, best friend, co-parent, problem solver, memory keeper, home organizer, planning partner, and teammate. I stopped wearing all of those hats when my marriage ended, but external hope allowed me to take them off the shelf once in a while, put them on, and breathe into the comfort of who I once was.

As you find yourself donning these old hats, even briefly, you'll notice the familiarity of your old roles returning. Depending on your loss, it's likely that the responsibilities you once held in your relationship are no longer the same. So, while engaging in them may provide you a sense of normalcy and even a reprieve from grief, it isn't best for your well-being. For instance, if you're estranged from your grandchildren, you may long to wear your grandparent hat near the holidays. You plan and prepare for your shared holiday traditions as you once did, and that familiarity helps you to feel good. You might tell yourself anything is possible, that your family may have a change of heart and show up as they once did. But when that doesn't happen, your pain is compounded, their absence amplifies your loss, and the hole in your soul hurts even more. In this way, external hope acts as a portal, allowing ambiguous grievers brief transport back to an old role and the relationship you once loved. As tempting at it is, there are healthier hats you can try on that won't keep you spinning in external hope. Here are a few things to keep in mind as you find them.

1. Simply recognizing your own experience can help you to make another choice. When you find yourself longing for the familiarity of what once was, acknowledge the desire to don your old role. The grandparent might say, "I long to host everyone for our annual day of holiday candy making, but I know that it's not in my control if they come." Allowing yourself to express both your desire and your reality is important as you work toward recovery.

2. Consider creating a new tradition, one that doesn't underscore what's absent but still brings you joy. The

grandparent might retire candy-making day and instead earmark that time for a new tradition: delivering toys to the children's hospital or shopping for a family in need.

3. Plan for your new activity in advance. If appropriate, invite others to join you and prepare accordingly. Enjoy the anticipation of the upcoming outing or activity and allow yourself to feel good during it. For example, pay attention to the joy you are bringing others, and be sure to accept their appreciation, too.

Such new roles usher in a deeper acceptance of life as it is now, not as it once was. Whether your excursions with external hope are frequent or occasional, each time you turn your energy in its direction, you're casting a line into the past and to a relationship that no longer lives as it once did. With one exception.

Depending on your activating event, this doesn't mean that you cannot create a new, healthy relationship with the person you're grieving. For some, ambiguous grief is experienced when the relationship changes in a normal and expected timeline, but the griever experiences a loss of their own identity. Take, for example, empty nesters, especially those who were the primary caretaker of the home and children. After two decades of an identity tied to the role of parent, it can be a jarring transition when you're no longer needed as you once were. While you may feel longing for the "good old days," acknowledging your feelings and shifting your perspective may help. While your adult children no longer need you to tuck them in at night, they still need you—just in different ways. By resisting the urge to dust off your parent hat, you create an opportunity to get to know your children as the adults they've become. This allows you both to create new shared experiences together and build a new relationship without lugging around the ball and chain of the old.

Whether or not you are continuing in relationship with your loved one, the more you practice shifting out of external hope, the more you'll generate chances to choose internal hope. For me, the more I could spot myself in external hope, the sooner I could make that shift. Ultimately, my perspective shifted formidably, and I began to think of myself not in relation to who I was to others—a mother, daughter, friend, and so on—but as a single, uniquely whole being, a middle-aged woman with blank pages of life left to write. Like many ambiguous grievers, at this point, I was excited and terrified at once. I didn't know how I was going to do it, but I was willing to bet on myself to figure it out.

And I did.

## The Next Right Thing

Making a commitment to go all in on yourself and rethinking what you want for your life may feel strange at first. It may be an unnerving task because parts of you may feel as though you are betraying a part of yourself or your former relationship, especially if you had a habit of putting the needs of others ahead of your own.

In my case, I was letting go of my old life and stepping into a new one—and I had no idea what I wanted it to look like. So, I adopted a mantra I learned at The Meadows and later learned is widely taught in AA meetings: do the next right thing. Sometimes the next right thing is to take a nap, and sometimes it's to take a chance. For me, at the altar of internal hope, it was to begin *life visioning*, a new-to-me concept from one of my favorite spiritual teachers, Dr. Michael Bernard Beckwith. After finishing his book by the same name, I began to practice "seeing" my future in my mind's eye, collecting images that hadn't yet happened: me running on a beach, healthy and strong; laughing with my children, all of us happy; feeling proud of my work, making meaningful contributions to my community; summiting Yosemite's Half Dome; even climbing to Mount Everest's Base Camp; and—the most difficult of them all—being held by a man with strong arms and a beautiful soul.

I would spend time with these images each day, sitting quietly, focused on each vision until I could feel it as if it were already happening for me. I loved how this felt and grew hungry for more. I began following my curiosities and questions on a broad range of topics by reading books, listening to podcasts, and watching interviews. This nourished me, mind, body, and soul. I was living in internal hope and starting to see a new life for myself—and I liked what I saw.

We'll explore this at out next stop, because I think you might like it for yourself, too.

## WISE WORDS ON HOPE AND PERSONAL POWER

"Hope is a form of planning."

—GLORIA STEINEM

"What, then, is to be done? To make the best of what is in our power and take the rest as it naturally happens."

—EPICTETUS

"God, grant me the serenity to accept the things I cannot change, the courage to change the things I can, and the wisdom to know the difference."

—"THE SERENITY PRAYER," REINHOLD NIEBUHR

"Fear can hold you prisoner. Hope can set you free."

—STEPHEN KING

## CHAPTER 4

# Internal Hope, Imprisonment, and What Elsa Forgot

"The secret of change is to focus all your energy
not on finding the old, but on building the new."
— DAN MILLMAN

"A Satyagrahi does not abandon his path, even
though at times it seems impenetrable and beset
with difficulties and dangers, and a slight departure
from that straight path may appear full of promise."
— GANDHI

Shortly before his second imprisonment in 1921, Mahatma Gandhi, leader of India's nonviolent campaign for independence from British rule, appealed to his followers to remain steadfast in their commitment to peaceful protests. As the movement escalated into a new phase, one marked by increased force from the British, he wrote of his personal experience in the newsletter *Young India*: "The spirit in me pulls one way, the flesh in me pulls in the opposite direction. There is freedom from the action of these two forces, but that freedom is attainable only by slow and painful stages. I cannot attain freedom by a mechanical refusal to act, but only by an intelligent action in a detached manner."[1]

The period you are entering in your ambiguous grief journey also offers the tantalizing taste of freedom, also realized only by persisting through slow and painful stages. That's because internal hope is cultivated through self-focus, and in order to practice self-focus and cast our attention to our new path, we have to let go and detach from the old. To take intelligent action in a detached manner, as Gandhi advises, you may have to live differently than before. This likely requires intentionally changing your behaviors and engaging your full self in the process. It is not simply enough to declare that you are choosing internal hope; like all declarations of merit, yours must be accompanied with immediate action. Gandhi didn't just declare a nonviolent campaign against British rule and expect to be granted freedom. He and his followers, called satyagrahis, took action by enduring prison sentences and hard labor camps and enacting public hunger strikes. This movement itself wasn't enough to actualize a different future; after all, declarations are just statements, even when accompanied by ceremonial signings or public attention.

The fate of any declaration depends on your sustained subsequent action or lack thereof. If you want or need to have more money in your bank account, you might declare, "I'm tired of living paycheck to paycheck!" But in order to change your situation, you have to support your declaration with action. Perhaps you find ways to increase your earnings or implement a plan to reduce your spending—or better yet, both! Otherwise, without that action, "I am tired of living paycheck to paycheck" isn't a declaration, it's just a desire.

While you won't have to engage in a battle with a global superpower like Gandhi did, you will have to take concrete action to bring a life of internal hope from a *declared desire* within you to a *practiced reality* around you. Now is the time to start walking your new path, making internal hope not only a declaration, but a **declaraction**.

It won't be easy, but it will be worth it!

## IT'S TIME TO ACT

You've already taken action by reading this book, but simply learning how others navigate their situation won't change yours, so further action is required of you. Establishing your mindset is a good first step of declar*action*, one Epictetus offers in the final line of his first principle: "If it concerns anything beyond your power, be prepared to say that it is nothing to you."

Let's unpack this. For me, this read as a dramatic, over-the-top directive, both emotionless and extreme—a black-or-white edict beyond necessity. Essentially, Epictetus is saying "put it out of your mind and never think of it again." However, after reflection on the extended amount of time I spent suffering in the "gray," I came to understand it differently. Just as sobriety cannot be claimed from a place of denial, so, too, joy cannot be claimed if you're still suffering in loss. So it is not enough to hope or wish to find joy again; instead, you'll need a commitment to your reality and to the action of creating it for yourself. I take umbrage with Epictetus's directive on this because to say "it is nothing to you" doesn't honor your loved one or the relationship you once shared, and I don't think we need to throw the baby out with the bathwater. To offer him a grand assumption, perhaps he never intended that line be applied to human relationships— or maybe he did, but his experience with grief does not appear to have been ambiguous. In that case, for those viewing this principle through the lens of love and loss, a slightly altered context may help:

> "If it concerns anything beyond your power, be prepared to say that ~~it is nothing to you~~ you choose yourself."

Choosing yourself may be a radical departure from your character or a dormant side to your personality, but cultivating this practice is key to successfully navigating this stage. To help internalize this concept, you can watch (or, more likely, rewatch) it in action during the final minutes of the blockbuster film *Titanic,* where Rose, in a last-ditch effort to return to a retreating lifeboat, takes action by plunging into the icy water and to a deceased passenger's frozen, but still working, whistle. This poignant scene shows what it looks like to take actionable commitment and choose yourself. Rose made a heartbreaking choice in a matter of seconds and said goodbye to her loved one in equal time. This portrays to us that the excruciating decision to let go of what was, or what could have been, is the only way to save yourself.

While we have established that holding on hurts and that we find relief when we can let go, that's far easier said than done. In Chapter 5, I'll introduce some actions that honor your loved one and the relationship you once shared. But before we can do that, let's spend time just on you, sharpening the tools you've already acquired and adding new ones to help form the new habit of choosing yourself. And if you truly want to go on, unlike Rose, you will have to choose yourself over and over again because, unlike her, your loved one is still living.

## SELF-FOCUS

Depending on how long you've been grieving, it's likely you've been told that you need to let go. Maybe like me, you have even offered the same lame "advice" to others before you knew better. When a caring person in my life imparted this insight to me a year into my grief, I responded with mock gratitude. "Oh, okay. That's all I need to do to feel better?

Wow, thank you." When I pressed him on how exactly to do this, he shrugged; he didn't know. How could he, when it was never something he'd had to do himself?

Though this exchange lasted less than a minute, it sparked my interest in the "how" of healing. I began turning the question back onto other well-meaning people who counseled me to "let go" or insinuated my grief was going on a bit too long. The most popular answers to my returned question of "how" were largely unhelpful. There were suggestions for faux actions that led to unanswerable questions (e.g., Friend: "Just don't think about it." Me: "Okay, how do I do that?"). Or there were the "stuffers," who advised me to heal by replacing the relationship or silencing my feelings via a myriad of unhelpful means. In both cases, this well-intended advice revealed unspoken commentary on the speed of my healing: if I could hurry it along, please and thank you, it would be more comfortable for everyone.

---

*Traveler's Tip: Beware the Worst Advice*

1. Move on
2. Just forgive them
3. Don't think about it
4. Don't talk about it
5. Pray it away

---

### *The How*

We talk of it for ourselves, encourage it for others, and even sing about doing it, but like grief itself, "letting go" is yet another aspect of loss that our society understands in theory but misses the mark on in execution. In 2013, we were singing about it collectively thanks to the animated film *Frozen*. A 2019 study[2] by the digital music service Spotify found "Let It Go" had become the most popular Disney song of all time, and today, with 300 million plays on Spotify alone, it's evident the song appeals to a broad audience. It's a catchy tune with affirming lyrics about embracing oneself and one's personal power, so it's no wonder the message resonates globally.

While the message is clear, once again, the implementation is not. I get it—we need to let go to move forward—but how? Elsa doesn't so much as hint as to how, not in this song or in the movie sequel (I know because I bought it just to find out).

### *Attach, Detach*

My search for "the how" led me to attachment theory, which proposes that interactions with caregivers during the first few years of life are a determining factor to developing one of four styles of attachment: secure, insecure anxious, insecure avoidant, or disorganized. These attachment styles then influence our adult relationships. Further, a growing body of research on attachment theory suggests that it also is a variable in understanding how we interact in personal relationships, from the bedroom to the boardroom. Whether you are self-confident, untrusting, clingy, tolerant, dismissive, have a fear of abandonment, or consider yourself to be emotionally self-sufficient, learning about your own attachment style may be helpful in understanding yourself and how you experience grief.

By that rationale, perhaps our attachment style holds clues to how we are grieving and may help to inform our detachment style as well. In moving through your ambiguous grief, the goal isn't to live attached and engaged, or detached and disengaged, but to shift your attachment into neutral. This helps to cultivate a feeling of gratitude for what is and will help you become more outcome-independent along the way. For me, this was supported by centering my energy around what was in my power as I began to pursue areas of self-focus. I spent less time and energy focused on my old relationship and I practiced being okay with the outcome, meaning I could find enjoyment in the experience of something without trying to force or will a desired outcome. In relation to the attachment to my former relationship, I found that structuring how and when I interacted with my loved one and others in my marital orbit helped me to detach and release my desire for any specific outcome to any particular interaction. Or, as we saw with Beth as she cared for her mother with Alzheimer's (see page 32), she let go of the desire to share honest family updates with her mother, since saying life was anything less than "good" proved to be too distressing for her mother to process. Such a shift allowed for detachment from the past relationship and made space for the new dynamic, one where the simple answer "good" removed unnecessary stress for them both.

## THREE TOOLS

While I never found an established prescription for letting go, I did discover some things that helped me more than others. My research project centered on hope helped me glean insights from survey answers and soon began to connect some interesting patterns. Letting go was an action-oriented process, I found. Through my own trial and error—combining breadcrumbs, adapting established techniques, and creating my own—I established three practical tools that helped me take action and walk the talk of my declaration of self-focus: the *rules of disengagement, soul salve,* and *future feeling.*

These three "how to" tools have helped me time and again, most significantly in the early days post-declaration. You're going to need all three in your backpack, so now is a good time to pause and remove any unnecessary weight or anything taking up space (e.g., resentment, bitterness, hostility, or anything Epictetus would deem not in your power). Don't worry if anything finds its way back inside—just keep removing it until it's gone for good!

## RULES OF ENGAGEMENT

When we are fiercely attached to something, whether it's a way of thinking or being in the world, or how we view ourselves or another person, it's likely we're restricting the possibilities for other thoughts to also be true. If you believe that you cannot be happy without your loved one as they once were, then you will not be open to the idea of receiving happiness in other ways. Just as your time and activities together helped to create the feelings of attachment to or dependency on your loved one, consciously engaging the opposite behavior will help to reframe and release that attachment and dependency. Of course, emotional detachment looks different for everyone, so creating some guidelines will help.

More than organizing and implementing boundaries, the ROD is a heartfelt framework that reflects your way of being in this new phase of your life. I adapted a rules of engagement (ROE) format to help guide me out of attachment and dependency on old patterns. Used throughout corporate America and by global militaries alike, the *Oxford English Dictionary* defines *rules of engagement* as a term used to describe directives issued by an authority specifying the circumstances and limitations under which forces will engage the enemy in combat. ROE documents do not define how a result is to be achieved, but what is and is not acceptable in attaining the desired outcome (e.g., soldiers have the right to defend themselves against an attack, or soldiers may not seize the property of others). In recent years, businesses have adopted the concept to guide workplace interactions as well.³ For example, ROE guidelines might establish that team members will respect confidentiality or will actively listen without interrupting.

## Rules of Disengagement

While your loved one may not be an enemy or an employee, this model can be adopted as a way to guide and actualize your physical and emotional detachment. Think of it as your rules of disengagement (ROD), a personalized plan that outlines the circumstances, events, and measures that are appropriate to help guide interactions with your loved one. Like a traditional ROE outline, the ROD does not seek to dictate how you achieve something; rather, it outlines what measures are permissible.

If your loved one was a romantic partner, you may have had a form of ROE at the onset of your attachment. Though likely unwritten, the framework may have included rules for your courting, such as how much time together was permissible, what events merited chaperones, or under what circumstances marriage would be considered. These guidelines may have been suggested by your partner, determined by you, enforced by your parents, influenced by religious beliefs, dictated by cultural norms, or simply understood between the two of you. Had you expanded on that unwritten framework, ROE might have detailed your curfew times, approved outing locations, or even financial savings goals; all are means of pacing intimacy and attachment.

By that rationale, applying ROD as a framework to enable and support distance and detachment may prove helpful. Some guidelines for disengagement could include:

- the right to remove myself from a hostile environment
- the right to keep myself physically and emotionally safe
- the right to decline activities or outings
- the right to redefine myself without outside permission
- the right to decide and own my feelings
- the right to defend myself from false or attempted attacks on my character
- the right to respond only when *not* doing so negatively impacts myself or others

Activating the guidelines of your ROD time and again will enforce the creation of new habits and support the construction of a new routine. This is hard enough, so be prepared to catch and correct yourself if you discover that you are mindlessly acting with spite or hostility. This may present in ways that include making disparaging or derogatory comments about your loved one, withholding or controlling behaviors, or blaming, shaming, or lying. All are rooted in fear, and ultimately imprison us in a victim mentality where we wallow in anger and a perceived unfairness of the situation. To counteract our fear and minimize such acting out, it may help to avert hostility by setting an intention to detach with love and abide by your ROD in a way that honors both the relationship you are grieving and yourself. For example, if you choose not to respond to unkind texts from your loved one, even though you might want to, you can remind yourself how you are honoring yourself in this action.

This doesn't mean that you don't have love for them, but that in your action you are choosing to act in honor and love for yourself.

It may help you to say a prayer for your loved one, meditate in loving awareness, or simply repeat a mantra. For me, I found "Love them, bless them, let them go" to be actionable, affirming, and self-fulfilling.

---

### Exercise 14 | *Create Your Rules of Disengagement*

The goal is to detach with love, so use simple, neutral language as much as possible. Ultimately, your ROD should be broadly stated boundaries, but if it helps you to get specific, please do! Remember, the examples I give aren't applicable to all activating events, so use them as your own if it suits you, but be sure to include a few of your own as well.

- Broad: I have the right to use my best judgment when interacting.
- Specific: I have the right to use my best judgment when my loved one is triggered and their behavior becomes aggressive toward me.

---

### Changing the Station

Like me and Maya from the desert, you may feel bouts of guilt that you are somehow "giving up" on your loved one, or, after focusing on their needs for so long, you may feel selfish as you pivot to focus more on your own. What I found, though, is that this is not "giving up" on a loved one or a lost relationship, but rather "giving your all" to a changed life for *you*.

I found that same spirit in a woman named Tameka, who, like Rose, made a decision to give her all to a life she never imagined. A vibrant and outgoing woman in her thirties, Tameka was living what she describes as a "happy life." She had earned a master's degree, landed her dream job, and, soon after, met the man she would marry. Life was "normal," Tameka told me, until one phone call changed everything.

Her husband had called to say that he was in trouble and had been arrested. "At first, I was relieved to hear from him," she told me, "because, by this time, we had a toddler and I was five months pregnant. I had spent several hours worrying because I hadn't been able to reach him, and he hadn't been home when I expected him. But as he was talking, I couldn't make sense of his words. I was overwhelmed and in shock. He was charged and held while we waited to learn the ruling and if, and for how long, he'd be sentenced. This [period of] time is known as pre-sentencing, and I was filled with anxiety—it was just waiting, waiting, waiting, to finally be told how long you have to wait!"

Tameka hoped her husband's sentence would bring relief with a ruling that would "allow him to come home, where everything would be okay again." But that didn't happen—her husband was sentenced to ten years in prison.

"He assumed I'd send him divorce papers, but I didn't. We had a good relationship, and I loved him, and so there was no urge for me to do that." Still, she wasn't sure how their marriage could survive under the new circumstances. Faced with the task of reconciling her new reality, Tameka felt angry and powerless as she worked to adapt to life with her husband behind bars. "I even felt guilty, wondering if I could have done something different," she said, "but I had to make my peace...what was done was done, and this is where we are."

Soon she was living her own sentence as a single, stressed-out, working mother of two and was responsible for supporting their family, from household bills to spending money for visits to the prison commissary. Feeling guilty for purchases that were once the norm, Tameka said, "items like scented bath soap suddenly felt like a luxury I couldn't afford and didn't deserve, so I wouldn't even allow myself that."

Tameka left her nine-to-five job in favor of a more flexible work schedule that she could control, one that better accommodated her new situation, but as a personal trainer and health instructor, the cost of that flexibility came in the form of a longer workday, with 4 a.m. to 9 p.m. "shifts" being common. A year into her "prison wife life," Tameka was suffering—exhausted and struggling with depression, grieving the loss of her relationship as it had been, and facing an unknown future ahead—when another defining moment changed her life yet again.

"It was a simple but powerful moment," Tameka said. "I looked at my son, and he looked like he had the world on his shoulders. Right then, I saw it: he is my reflection. He looked sad and stressed…his father is incarcerated, he's cared for by a single, depressed mother, and he's a Black boy, and that is hard enough. So, right then, I made the decision to change me. I started on a new path and changed the radio station; literally that was the first thing I did that changed my environment. I turned the dial and filled my ears with positive words, and it started me on a whole new path."

Until that point, Tameka had been consumed with her own grief and caring for everyone but herself, focused on the hardship of her reality and circumstances she couldn't change. Though she couldn't see where the long and lonely road as a prison wife was going to take her, Tameka became committed to at least being the one in the driver's seat. "I was determined to teach my boys that no matter what happens in their lives, they can still rise, they can still be successful."

She set a big goal herself: to get in her best shape and register for a fitness competition. Though she already had little time for herself, she was determined to find a way to bring action to her deeply rooted desire. Tameka registered for the competition and committed to her goal, five minutes at a time, for months. "For my mental health, I absolutely had to, and even though my husband didn't understand why I did it, or necessarily like that I did it, I had to pursue that desire in my heart. He respected that."

In this way, Tameka chose to have hope for herself. She said, "In order for me to support anyone else, I had to do this for me."

Today, Tameka is a coach to spouses and partners of incarcerated loved ones, helping them embrace the choices they have and claim their power by making decisions for themselves. "I tell them, don't put your life on hold while he's away. Go finish that degree or start the business, start dreaming and doing, and don't feel guilty for doing it, either. I held boundaries with everyone around me, including my husband, too. I knew he was hurting, and I wanted to be his rock, but some days doing that would have cost me my goal. It wasn't my job to take on his problems, it was my job to solve my own—and I did."

---

## SOUL SALVE

In my case, embracing self-focus wasn't helped along by a physical goal like Tameka's. Though I had once loved swimming, biking, and running, any physical activity beyond gentle walking had proven difficult in the first year and a half after my activating event, requiring more energy than I had to give. This is a common experience for grievers and makes sense when we consider that grief is not only emotional but a physical experience as well. Specifically, the body's response during bereavement includes, among other things, an elevation of the stress hormone cortisol, which impacts both our immune system and cardiovascular system. With my body perpetually aching, I instead focused on learning new things and training my brain. By getting quiet and present in my daily meditation, I was able to identify what my soul needed— and it wasn't a new handbag or a new husband, a martini or a makeover, but a deeply rooted desire to feel smart. I became particularly obsessed with TED Talks, learning about topics that made me think, sparked wonder, and helped me laugh. I felt at ease every time I'd read a book about grief and find within it some nugget of understanding.

While I caught myself cycling in and out of external hope (remember, it happens!), I also noticed how my grief would retreat, if only a little bit, when I focused on me and was engaging in activities that led to my growth. I didn't realize it at the time, but this "intellectual binge" was a vital component of my healing. When I found out my former husband was not who I'd known him to be, I felt duped. I felt pretty dumb for not recognizing traces of his duplicity sooner. Loading up on learning helped me to activate a curious part of myself that had gone dormant in the wake of my grief, and I couldn't get enough of it. My living room doubled as both library and lecture hall, a place where I read countless books and watched every *Super Soul Sunday* broadcast. These were the early actions that supported my commitment to self-focus and moved me forward toward recovery.

Focusing internally costs nothing and is accessible to almost everyone; all you have to do is nourish parts of yourself that need care. Your intellect can be fed by watching documentaries, listening to podcasts, and reading books. Your creative side can sparkle again by learning something new, such as playing an instrument, painting, or coding, or taking up a hobby like cooking or doing puzzles. Your desire to be of service can be met by helping a family member or neighbor, volunteering, or becoming involved in groups that share your passions like art, reading, or community service. Or, like Tameka, your motivation may lie in strengthening your physical body, and training for a competition may prove the perfect balm for your soul. No matter what it is, choosing how to soothe your soul is filed in the "within your power" folder. But you first have to get quiet and tune in to what it is your soul needs. For those of us willing to indulge the still, small voices of our higher selves, this action of listening and answering allows us to begin tapping into our individual gifts, awakening our dormant dreams, and envisioning a new life for ourselves.

## FUTURE FEELING

As you practice self-focus and find what soothes your soul, you may discover twinges of optimism. For some, this is your innate state of being, but for others it may feel entirely foreign, even alarming. That's normal because, with sustained focus on you, you're changing. Whether you have adopted a new daily routine or found free time you haven't had before, the action produces the outcome. For instance, maybe you're now exercising before breakfast, meditating midday, or stopping at the farmer's market instead of the quickie mart. Perhaps you are pruning your newly planted flower garden of unhealthy friendships, planting seeds for new ones to grow. Change doesn't hurt forever, and like that bulb buried underground, when hope does finally spring internally, optimism may bloom with it. It might catch you off-guard because it hasn't been your experience for some time, if ever, but if you can allow yourself to see the good in whatever way optimism is showing up, it might just surprise you!

One of the ways your self-focus practice may begin to bear fruit is in the burgeoning form of affirming feelings. As you become reacquainted with joy, laughter, optimism, and internal hope, affirm these moments of growth with gratitude. Giving thanks for every little thing that brought me joy during this time had a delightful effect; it seemed to not only multiply the long-lost sparkly feelings, but enable me to consume them as if each time were the first time. These feelings felt acutely potent, buzzing through me as intensely as my first-ever cup of espresso. If you wake up in the morning, give gratitude before you even get out of bed, and return gratitude to whatever gives you joy throughout the day, you'll watch it multiply. For me, this sounded like, "Thank you, coffee," after the morning's first sip. "Thank you, lungs," at the end of a walk. "Deep gratitude, dear friend," to the soul sister who had me howling with laughter. "I'm so grateful, pizza delivery," for bringing our family dinner so quickly! A surrender to your state of joy (no matter how fleeting), coupled with authentic, abundant gratitude, will ready you for activating the process of "future feeling."

This is a daily practice that builds upon the gifts of gratitude and the warm, fuzzy physical sensations it brings. Future feeling is a short and intentional act of visualizing that helps you to begin to imagine your new life by feeling it. This meditative practice connects you to a yet-to-be experienced version of yourself by tapping into a heartfelt desire in your mind's eye and then sitting with that vision until your body can feel it as though it's happening in the present. For me, this became a deeply personal activity that allowed me to reimagine my life in a way that was comfortable and empowering. After months of sustained focus on the present moment as part of my healing, future feeling was also a welcome reprieve, an opportunity to relax my mind, tune in to the deepest part of me, and briefly focus on my future. The focus isn't on any specific point in time, like next Friday or your milestone birthday, but simply a time that has yet to happen.

Depending on the nature of your activating event, you may feel vulnerable allowing yourself to feel internal hope, joy, or optimism, and that's understandable. Use your "preacting" tool (see page 42) to get behind the thought driving that feeling. Work through that until you ground yourself in the present moment. Then, you're ready to work toward your future feeling.

## Exercise 15 | It's Time to Reimagine

It's time to pause and focus on *you*. Get quiet, tune in, and ask your heart these inspiring questions about your future. Seek out your own intuition, your "knowing." Try not to judge your answers or dismiss them. Write them down as they arise in your awareness. You can check your answers against your gut instinct to determine whether these are the true answers from your deepest self or a filtered or edited version from your ego. Rework them until they feel authentic to your soul—that part of you that is your best, loving self. Hold the image until you can feel it, and follow the feeling as it reverberates through you.

1. What do I see myself doing?
2. With whom do I want to spend time?
3. How do I express my soul self?
4. What gifts do I hold within me that will be shared?
5. What do I need to set free to live my new life?

As you begin to recognize your answers as the truth from within you and not your ego, start to get acquainted with how they *feel*. Don't try to set the stage and fill in specifics; seeing the details isn't as important as the feeling. Hold on to that feeling for at least fifteen seconds, letting the feeling wash through you as though it is happening. For example, feel what it is like as your gifts and talents are appreciated and valued by others. Notice how it feels throughout your body as you hold that vision. Sometimes, you may feel uncomfortable with what your intuition reveals (e.g., you're with the wrong partner or in the wrong job, or not acknowledging the truth about something, etc.), so pay attention to those feelings just as you do those that are comfortable or inviting. As I practiced holding the feeling of my intuition, whether it was comfortable or not, I became more attuned to the affirming feelings I preferred and grew keenly aware of who and what in my life aligned with this feeling. As a result, I became more discerning about how and with whom I interacted. This kind of relationship reckoning can be difficult—it was for me—but minimizing interaction with that which feels unaligned is necessary in order to protect your own energy, whether that means removing yourself from a friend that drains you or the least-grumpy cashier at the grocery. Once this clicked, I understood that when I am protecting my energy and following the feelings born from my own intuition, I am on the path leading to the greatest and highest vision for my life.

For a deeper practice, I highly recommend "life visioning," a meditative practice outlined in the book *Life Visioning* by Dr. Michael Bernard Beckwith. The process hones your intuition through silent awareness and deep curiosity, connecting you to your soul and to the Divine. Asking empowering questions in my future feeling practice was inspired by Beckwith's work.

---

## Future Feeling Goggles

I also began to honor my intuition by incorporating "the lens technique," a technique Amy taught me. Especially helpful in growing empathy or in trying to learn how others view the world, simply applying a new lens to your own vantage point allows you to toggle between different perspectives. For instance, you can use an "anxiety lens" to better understand why a loved one with an anxiety disorder is behaving in a way you don't understand. If you seek to understand a behavior that is foreign to you and you are willing to learn about it, then try using that lens when you are stumped by or can't make sense of someone's behavior. I applied a "reimagining lens" to not only see but to feel and intuit the world around me in a new way. Through what I call my "goggles," I understood who and what was in alignment with the feeling trying to emerge within me. I bumped that feeling up against everything I encountered to test its orientation in my life; if the person, place, or purchase didn't line up with that feeling, then it wasn't meant for me. I found that what the Stoic style "sort and file" method does for the mind, the future feeling goggles trick does for the soul.

As I applied it more and more—saying YES to what served me and no to what didn't—I soon found myself living in that tingling sensation outside of my practice. I had surrounded myself with people, places, and practices with energy that aligned with my highest self. Fresh ideas, new understandings, and never-before-considered activities were happening within and around me. Some long-forgotten dreams awoke; dusty and stiff out of their decades-long hibernation, they whispered for my attention once more. Old memories bubbled up, too, like the time a well-meaning but careless adult posed that dreaded question, "What do you want to be when you grow up?"—then informed my eight-year-old self that writers "don't make any money" and suggested I rethink my response.

What was happening within and around me was happening for me. My grief wasn't gone, but it didn't consume me as it once did. It seemed ironic that I was in such a powerful state of feeling after being beleaguered by excruciating pain for so long, but this pain was a catalyst. My pain, not my joy, drove me to this very point in time, to a set of perfectly placed coordinates that I would never have known existed had my activating event not happened. It was then, as a new view for my life was taking shape, that pain passed my soul like a baton, with Olympic-level precision, into the outstretched and waiting grasp of possibility. As Dr. Beckwith so eloquently states, in this experience, "pain pushes until the vision pulls."

"Let go," said pain.

"Let's go!" said possibility.

"*Yes!*" I declared.

Like Tameka's decision to take action and turn the radio station, tuning in to a new frequency within myself shifted me as well. With a focus on self, boundary setting, and life-visioning, I was tuned in to a new frequency and receiving messages loud and clear. As you do the same, remember that change often happens over a lengthy period of time, in tiny shifts, small movements, and seemingly subtle activity. Compounded, these tiny adjustments yield mighty benefits, in the same way a straight and steady stream finds a way around obstacles, redirecting its flow time and again, persisting each day, and ultimately evolving into a roaring river and creating a new way ahead for itself.

As you connect to your own inner knowing, your intuition will pull you to learn more about what you need and make visible what is important around you. Pay attention to how you are feeling as you follow your own guidance, and be careful not to dismiss a feeling before you know for sure how it's presenting for you. Remember, feelings, emotions, and experiences all contribute to our emotional makeup and often overlap or confuse us with their commonalities. For example, before you dismiss your intuition because it brings about an experience of anxiety, take a closer look to be sure that's indeed the case. You might find that what you're feeling isn't anxiety, but excitement—two feelings that present alike but are derived from different thoughts. Further, you may even recognize a new feeling, but unless you investigate, you may not know how to file it. It could be warning you against something or signaling to you that your actions are in alignment to the highest, best part of yourself. But the more you practice tuning in to your intuition and allowing it to guide you, the more comfortable you'll be in trusting it and yourself.

It is in this way that I made peace with that part of myself, my "soul self," I initially and erroneously believed had failed me. In this meditative practice, the connection to myself strengthened, and I realized it had been there all along. It had never gone away or failed to alert me, it was I—the "me of the world" who had failed *it*. Just as scientists send messages into the cosmos and quarterbacks send passes down the field, an alert from within is only complete when it connects with a receiver. In understanding this, I set an intention to be such a receiver and not only tune in to my intuition, but trust it by taking action.

For me, my intuition guided me to documentaries and articles to learn about the varied healing modalities practiced around the world. Soon, I grew intrigued by cultures that seemed to celebrate loss and honor pain as part of the human condition. One specific tradition from the Amazon intrigued me beyond all others. After a month of learning, I wasn't just casually curious about it, but felt pulled to the experience of it. So, in the spirit of declar*action* and in a show of trust to my intuition, I committed to an act of internal hope my old self would have been hard-pressed to entertain. I traveled to deep in the Costa Rican jungle, where, under the care of the youngest shaman from the oldest tribe in South America, I sat in an ancient ceremony, during which I was forced to confront my beliefs and discovered answers to questions I hadn't known to ask. You don't have to travel to the jungle to heal, but if, in following your own intuition, it leads you there, and if it's in alignment with your integrity, I encourage you to consider it with an open mind.

## WISE WORDS ON ATTACHMENT AND ACTION

"In the end these things matter most: How well did you love? How fully did you live? How deeply did you let go?"

—JACK KORNFELD

"What we do is more important than what we say or what we say we believe."

—BELL HOOKS

"Do what you can, with what you've got, where you are."

—SQUIRE BILL WIDENER OF WIDENER'S VALLEY, VIRGINIA, FROM *THEODORE ROOSEVELT: AN AUTOBIOGRAPHY*

"It is not the mountain we conquer, but ourselves."

—SIR EDMUND HILLARY

"I had never thought about the fact that by getting locked up, I was also imprisoning everyone who loved or cared about me."

—SHAKA SENGHOR, *WRITING MY WRONGS*

## CHAPTER 5

# The Bridge to Recovery, Addiction, Reconciliation, and Rituals

"When one has nothing left make ceremonies out of the air and breathe upon them."
—CORMAC MCCARTHY, *THE ROAD*

"The road we travel is equal in importance to the destination we seek. There are no shortcuts. When it comes to truth and reconciliation, we are forced to go the distance."
—JUSTICE MURRAY SINCLAIR

"Pain is a hot potato," Amy told me in one of my many therapy sessions. "We don't want to hold it, so we look for the person who threw it to us and want to throw it back at them. Throwing it back, that is blame."

"Okay, but I didn't ask for the hot potato in the first place," I countered, "the potato isn't my fault, and I didn't deserve it, either."

Amy nodded at my argument and then shrugged.

"You can just drop it though, right?"

Whatever, Amy.

As you travel the path of internal hope, you should start feeling stronger and better able to understand your grief. Through your continued practice of self-focus, you are getting to know yourself again, and through declar*action*, you are activating new parts of yourself, too. By now, you are naming your feelings, observing your thoughts, and honoring your boundaries. All of this results in your spending fewer days in external hope and less time cycling. You're interacting with the world again, in a healthy way, and as you emerge from this leg of your journey, you may even be starting to feel more like yourself, too. This isn't to say you aren't still grieving, but your grief is likely starting to change form; maybe you feel its assaults less frequently or with less intensity. Although you're closer to recovery than you've ever been, ambiguous grief continues to ask more.

Before you move ahead, it's time to check your emotional pockets for any remaining "hot potatoes." As Amy described, pain is a like a hot potato, and in your case, it hurts because it came from someone you love. Though our response is often to relieve the pain by throwing back, many of us hold on to it instead. As we hold that hot potato, we bear more pain, which becomes our suffering. If you want to cross the void between your grief and recovery, you'll need to release your suffering along the way; you'll need to drop the hot potato. To help you do so, you will need another tool to move you through this passage, and, unlike the others thus far, this is one tool that you must forge yourself. This tool will help you move out of suffering but will require your imagination and all the emotional energy you can muster.

In reflecting on my own experience at this point, and in bearing witness to others who have arrived here, a common denominator stands out: we are tired. You likely feel emotionally exhausted and physically drained, if not both, but remember, this is a normal reaction to grief and mourning. Just think about all you have already endured—the whirlwind of a life-changing activating event, a ride on a nonstop roller coaster through the stages of grief, and a game of Whack-a-Mole with hope, the double agent who misdirected your focus. Finding signs of peace and comfort (at last!) through the repetition of internal hope practices, it's understandable that you are ready to rest—not perform the added labor of building a proverbial bridge. But in order to transport yourself from your old life and into your new in a healthy fashion, you first have to conquer the daunting task of reconciling the two. Reconciliation doesn't mean restoring your relationship to its previous state; I'm not suggesting you reunite with the partner who betrayed you, ignore your parent's cognitive decline, or dismantle the healthy boundaries you've built for yourself. Not in the least. In this context, reconciliation is the ability to honestly identify and accept the relationship both for what it once was and what it is now. Think of reconciliation like an ampersand (&) joining two separate things and making them whole. In reconciliation, you hold both the past & the present relationship simultaneously in a defining, self-constructed awareness that joins the end of the old with the start of the new.

If this sounds exhausting and you need to set your backpack down and rest, by all means do! Just be careful of the alluring old adage that "time heals." While that may hold some truth, too much time in a state of inaction can tempt you into complacency.

It might be difficult to visualize how to reconcile your loss and integrate your "old & new" relationship, especially if you've never done the emotional work of integrating conflicted feeling or belief systems. But it can be done! Thanks to written records, oral stories, and archaeological discoveries, we know there are tools that have served as helpful aides to humankind throughout history. They have taken on many forms over time and continue to assist our transitions in innumerable ways. At their core, they allow us to honor the past and have gratitude for the now. The time-tested tools of ceremony and ritual are the chief instruments needed for building your bridge of reconciliation. I recognize that my own experiences shared in this chapter may raise an eyebrow, and I encourage you to look past that, to the benefits of ceremony and ritual above all else. I'm sharing two that were of personal benefit to me; one with ancient roots spanning generations, and the other created by myself, for myself. While both proved an important part of my path, only you can determine what will be part of yours.

## TOOLS OF THE TRADE: RITUAL AND CEREMONY

Regardless of upbringing, it's likely you've participated in a variety of rituals and ceremonies throughout your lifetime. Though the terms are often confused or used interchangeably (like "feelings" and "emotions"), their differences are important to understand. Think of a ceremony as an event performed in honor of something special, like a birthday party or wedding, while a ritual is an action or group of actions, like singing the happy birthday song, blowing out candles, and eating cake. You may ritualize the end of the workweek by ordering pizza every Friday night, or bedtime by repeating the same prayer before you get into bed. Rituals don't have to be part of a ceremony, but most ceremonies include rituals; for example, when people get married, the wedding is the ceremony, while the recitation of vows and exchange of rings are the ritual. Although they aren't exclusive to practices of faith or religious experiences, many of these events are spiritual experiences, and the word itself suggests as much—*spiritual* is a ritual of the spirit. Whether in the form of a religious baptism or a daily soak in your bathtub, prayer with your higher power or communal sharing with Your People, rituals can serve as powerful healing aids. Expressed within a ceremony, these tools help us to organize, acknowledge, and honor our transitions.

With effort, intention, and a little imagination, constructing your own ceremony with rituals can help you to reconcile your reality and build a bridge to recovery in the process. My bridge was built in the most unlikely ways, its planks made of a variety of experiences—from violent vomiting in the jungle to songs on the shore of a small local lake, with a thousand bathtub prayers in between. This building isn't a fast process, but you aren't timed, and there is no reward for speed, so begin when you are ready and proceed at your own pace. The goal is to reconcile your reality for as long as you need to, in as many ways as you need to, however you need to. Eventually, you'll find yourself moving closer to recovery, and, one ceremonial plank at time, you will have built a sturdy bridge. For inspiration, let's explore some ways that ceremonies and rituals are performed around the world, starting with a South American healing ceremony that is currently growing in global popularity but has been performed by indigenous Amazonians for much of known human history.

## The Cave

High in the Andes mountains of southwest Bolivia, the gaping mouth of Cueva del Chileno (or "Chilean Cave") beckons from the face of an expansive rock wall, an open invitation to enter. Based on what's been unearthed inside, it's known that the natural formation has been entered by many, serving as both shelter and tomb for the last four thousand years. Situated among treacherous terrain at an elevation of nearly four thousand feet, it stands today as it has long been—the lone option for protection on a desolate and exposed mountainside. In 2010, an excavation of the site by a team of international archaeologists found clues about the cave's long line of inhabitants.[1]

At first glance, those excavating the site had reason to feel disappointed, discovering only the equivalent of "trash" left behind by decades-old cave robbers. However, on closer inspection, the dig team made a fantastic discovery: a sewn pouch made from three fox snouts containing a hand-carved spatula, a headband, and traces of two plants used in ritualistic healing ceremonies. Carbon dating placed the objects between AD 900 and AD 1170, which led the team to a compelling conclusion: this wasn't just an ordinary pouch—it was a shaman's medicine bag and is believed to be the earliest evidence of ayahuasca, a known psychoactive plant medicine administered only by tribal healers in ceremonies throughout South America. Ayahuasca is the same brew that was dispensed to me by an Incan-descended shaman a thousand years later as part of a sacred ritual that connected my present and past and helped me to reconcile my reality.

## The Jungle

As it turns out, the plants identified within the ancient shaman's pouch are still used today just as they appear to have been used then: to create a potent hallucinogenic brew known as ayahuasca. The ayahuasca drink is a decoction of two natural ingredients, most commonly made from "the bark of a vine named *Banisteriopsis caapi* (*B. caapi*) combined with the leaves of a DMT-containing plant, *Psychotria viridis*. Indigenous traditions consider the *B. caapi* vine to be the main ingredient of ayahuasca and name the brew after the native species."[2] When consumed, it accesses the central nervous system and activates an alternate state of consciousness. As I sought ways to manage my own grief and explored healing techniques, I read the personal testimonies of everyday people who found ayahuasca beneficial in easing many modern-day afflictions, including addiction, trauma, and grief. I grew curious about the medicine and what it might do for me. I was fascinated by its existence and by how, out of the tens of thousands of plant species in the rainforest, the region's indigenous people knew just which two exact components of two specific plants were needed to create such a complex and powerful medicine, one some describe as the greatest hallucinogenic we know. But on its own, this medicine is only half of the whole; the sacred ceremony and its rituals are the other. For that reason, it's important that drinking ayahuasca is experienced within the indigenous tradition under the guidance of a trained shaman. A 2021 study published in *Frontiers in Pharmacology* supports this, finding that participation in a ceremony, and specifically feeling supported and safe within a plant medicine ceremony, was "significantly associated with all outcomes in a beneficial direction, including a greater number of self-insights [and] stronger spiritual experience."[3] In other words: this is not a party drug. Don't try this at home!

Just as it's notorious for its medicinal power, the brew is also known for its undesirable taste. If I had to guess the recipe ingredients by taste alone, I would have thought it was made by mixing motor oil with a full ashtray and topping with a sprinkle of freshly cut pine. Not surprisingly, it induces purging in all forms, especially vomiting, but also defecating, belching, crying, laughing, and even hiccupping. Amazonian shamans teach that when we purge, we are expelling our unhealthy attachments: the thoughts, beliefs, or substances that do not serve us. That is why, two years following my activating event, I traveled to Costa Rica to sit in a shamanic-led ceremony with dozens of others. Less than an hour after my first drink, I was on my hands and knees (the preferred posture for purging—who knew?) violently heaving my insides into a plastic blue bucket, the kind you would use to mop your floor. I physically clung to "Blue" that night and the three nights following, as the shamans guided the plant medicine to work. If this sounds "out there" to you, I understand. It's how I felt at first, too, especially as someone whose drug use extended only to the use of the anti-anxiety medication and antidepressants introduced the year before. Mind-altering substances had never been of interest to me, but the more I learned about the ancient plant medicine, the deeper I grew in a knowing that it was something I had to do.

## THE LAUNCH

Many of our ceremonies include "helpers," like pallbearers at funerals, bridesmaids and ringbearers at weddings, and party guests at birthdays. It's this way with the ayahuasca ceremony as well. Like the shaman leading our ceremony, the helpers offer minimal intervention but are attuned to everyone's needs and act in support, replenishing tissues and monitoring movement. The helpers escorted us forward to the shaman, and, one by one, we whispered our intention into the small steeped liquid, then emptied our shot glass in one giant gulp.

Waiting for the ashtray taste to dissipate, I sat patiently under the partial roof of the ceremonial building known as a *maloca* and drank in the splendor of my surroundings, from unhampered views of the Milky Way above to peaceful sounds of nocturnal jungle birds outside. To my right, a twenty-something trauma survivor breathed deeply, trying in vain to steady her nerves. To my left, a bearded man in his forties told me that it was his third visit, that he was recovering from substance abuse, and that it would be okay. A guest of the bearded man sat opposite me. She met my eyes and I recognized her from the airport two days before. I had watched her as I waited for the resort shuttle to arrive and concluded she was either homeless or mentally ill. But as she frolicked barefoot in a small patch of grass meant for the relief of airplane-traveling animals, I determined that she was probably both. When she boarded the resort shuttle along with me and a handful of others, I felt immediately uneasy as she took her seat in the row behind me. Though I never turned around to look at her, I heard the hushed voices of her traveling companions comfort her soft whimpers until she fell asleep. "Addiction is the devil," someone said.

Now, as she sat across from me in an ayahuasca ceremony, I could see that her dark eyes sank deeply into her face. I realized that I knew her from somewhere, before seeing her in the airport. Scanning her for clues, I noticed her dirty feet were a stark contrast against the crisp white cotton bedsheet. She must have been aware of my judgmental thoughts because she quickly scurried into a new position, tucking her dirty feet behind her, out of my sight. She rose onto her folded knees and rocked herself ever so slightly. Her familiarity grew as I continued to watch her. I felt a pang of embarrassment when she caught me looking at her, but that evaporated as she held my stare. Neither of us looked away, so I mirrored her motion and rocked myself to her rhythm. As we self-soothed, separate yet together, all of her familiarity connected for me at once: she was me. With that, I was launched out of the jungle and into the vastness of generational galaxies.

"Addiction is the devil," I heard again.

## THE DARK FOREST OF ADDICTION

Back in suburban America, far from the jungle, Ilianna and Jim were dealing with the "devil" as well, but you wouldn't know it unless they told you. By all appearances, they were the perfect couple. Together since college, the sweethearts married, launched their respective careers, and started a family. A few years later, the perfect couple had grown a perfect family, complete with two sons, one daughter, and a playful pup. The images shared on social media were enviable, showing a gorgeous family playing together outdoors, dancing with one another among fallen leaves, and splashing in summer's sunshine. Their laughter is practically palpable through the screen, but it's a stark contrast to what Ilianna describes as she shares her story. What the snapshots do not reveal, she tells me, is a family recovering from the overwhelming impact of addiction.

"It really shocked me," Ilianna said. "Jim had always been responsible, and he really loved his job—he took a lot of pride in his work as a pharmacist. We dated for nine years, but it wasn't until four months after our wedding, when he was fired, that I learned the truth. It never remotely occurred to me that he had been abusing prescription drugs, but knowing what I do now, it makes perfect sense. Without an understanding of addiction, it was easy to miss."

It was an extremely difficult time, she told me, not only because her husband was reeling in shame from the exposure of his secret, but he was suffering through the painful symptoms of drug withdrawal, too. "I went into full-on fix-it mode," Ilianna said with a laugh, "and only now, as I look back, can I see how ridiculous it was that I thought I could fix anything." Like so many who experience the emotional impact of an activating event, her instincts took over, but more than fight or flight, her reaction was "fix."

She turned her focus to her husband and made a plan, ensuring Jim completed the two-year treatment intensive needed to retain his pharmacy license. In addition to self-reporting to a health professional recovery program administered by their state, Ilianna established rules and a daily schedule reporting to her as well. "By staying close, by managing him, like I thought I was, I felt that I had control over how this would play out. As long as I did that, I had hope I would get my husband back. But," Ilianna sighed, "it was false hope because he relapsed, and that's when I learned that you can't manage an addict. You can only manage yourself. Once this happened, I really started to grieve for everything that had been lost."

Many ambiguous grievers experience a strong desire to fix the problem threatening their relationship. This behavior is external hope in action; whether it's sourcing information to help our loved one, crafting communication on their behalf, controlling what information is released and to whom, or doing damage control, the person closest to the activating event often assumes a self-appointed role of "fixer." This makes sense because, even though we didn't "cause" the activating event, our life as we know it is at risk because of it. Ilianna took her fixing role seriously, acting as architect and advisor, but her valiant efforts were short-lived, and even had disastrous consequences of their own. "By the time he relapsed, we had started our family and had two of our kids. It was much worse for me this time," she shared. "I had gotten so sick, not just physically but mentally. I just couldn't wrap my head about how he could do this to our family, and I had a lot of resentment toward him."

A popular aphorism within the addiction recovery community is "We are only as sick as our secrets." But like many who are impacted by a loved one's addiction, Ilianna didn't know whom she could trust or confide in. "I felt shame and was too embarrassed to even tell anyone about it at first, especially my family and friends," she explained. "I told myself that I might share it after it was behind us, and that I was actually protecting everyone by keeping this private. But everything became so unmanageable—I was so focused on keeping him 'on track,' I was not focused at all on me. I didn't know what to do, but I knew I needed to get help for myself. I went to a Nar-Anon meeting, and that's when everything changed."

Modeled in the group meeting style of Alcoholics Anonymous, the Nar-Anon program is a worldwide fellowship for those affected by someone else's addiction. The program literature underscores that it is "not a religious but a spiritual way of life" that uses a twelve-step program and many other tools to enrich individual recovery. Ilianna described the ceremony of the meetings and the rituals: "The structure of the meetings is the same every week, but the topic and the sharing are different, and the sharing that happens at these meetings is really powerful. How we end each meeting is also special: we hold hands, recite the Serenity Prayer together, and then in unison say, 'Keep coming back! It works if you work it, and you're worth it!'

"At first, it felt a little hokey. But soon, everything about the meetings helped me. Even though the meetings were in a drafty church basement with dim lighting, I loved going into the room. In the beginning, I dreaded getting out of my car and going in—what if someone saw me? What if I went in and someone in there knew me? Then my secret would be out. Eventually, I realized that if they were in there seeing me, well, then I was seeing them, and we had something in common."

Slowly, Ilianna began to shed that shame by learning about substance and behavioral abuse disorders. She came to understand addiction not as a character flaw or moral failing, but as a medical condition that is likely tied to a genetic predisposition, early trauma, or both. "There was a *lot* of emotion in that room, and people come in at various stages of understanding," Ilianna said, recalling her first meetings. "There is certainly nothing glamorous about addiction or addiction support! But now I see these meetings as some of the most beautiful experiences in my life."

## THE STARS

Back in the jungle, with my soul deep in space and my head deep in my bucket, I thought of Wilson, the volleyball-turned-best-friend-to-Tom-Hanks in the film *Cast Away*. A flash of their oceanic separation panged me, so I clutched tighter: "Stay with me, Blue," I pleaded with a whisper-yell. I was soon enveloped by warmth, and I floated throughout space without fear. A familiar and friendly presence showed me around, slowing our speed to a stop so that I could take in the varying shades of darkness and notice the infinite layers of stars as they danced. Some stars were consistently bright and unmoving, some were pulsing with a motion like a heartbeat, and others sparked, zapping like an electric plug trying to connect into a faulty socket. I felt a "Zap!" sensation as I watched and understood that I was one of the frayed, zapping stars, unable to connect.

The loving energy showed me that each part of the darkness held a section of time that appeared only when I would fix my gaze upon it. As I comprehended this information, one area immediately opened and began playing a home movie of my life. I was starring in a documentary replaying my own memories, some that I'd long forgotten, and others I never even remembered yet knew to be true. I delighted in the viewing as a third-party observer. Then, zap! My point of view changed, and I would watch the same scenes from a first-person point of view inside some kind of container. While the container felt familiar, it wasn't my preferred perspective. My consciousness toggled between these two vantage points in space and the awareness of my body and its place in the jungle. I was aware of myself from all three perspectives: in the container floating in space, on the bed in Costa Rica, and as an observer learning from it all. What I saw through this variable view changed me forever: I simultaneously understood that the container was my body and that I was looking out from within it. In that instance I absorbed a never-before-experienced understanding of who I am.

> I am not my body. I am inside my body, and I exist
>   outside of it, too.
> I am both in my earthly body experiencing from this
>   perspective, and observing from a distance, taking
>   notes and learning.
> I am of the same loving energy that has been guiding
>   and teaching me.
> I am longing to connect; we are all longing to connect.
> The love we give and receive never leaves us; our love
>   connects us eternally.

I can hear the Girl giggling across from me, but I can't find her in the vastness of space. As I straddle both worlds, I feel the breeze from the shaman's leaved fan move over me and hear the helpers begin to welcome my fellow sojourners. I feel an explosion of love and understand that it is all the love I've ever known, all I've given and all I've received. I recognize the souls around me as my "earthly" loved ones, and what I sense between us is a breathtaking magnitude of love. There is no anger, animosity, regret, or resentment. There is no fear, only love. Love is all that remains and all that ever matters.

The warm, loving presence is still with me but is no longer guiding me where to go next. I understand that my lesson is nearing the end, and while I'm agreeable to leave, I don't know how. The Girl giggles again. I follow her laughter like light posts along a dark path. Though I don't see her in space, I feel her there with me, just as I know that she is there with me in the ceremony. One lamppost-like giggle at a time, her laughter begins to lead me out of space. Tears heave from my eyes—an amalgam of sorrow and celebration. As I purge through my tears, I am overwhelmed with both grief and gratitude, and with gratitude for my grief. I surrender to my truth; I want to fully plug in and connect and know that doing so restores a gift inherent in all of us, one that once discovered can never be lost: unconditional love.

Like a dam that simply can no longer withstand the force of a raging river, I break. An endless wave of liquid love bursts from a reservoir deep within me, escaping as twin rivers rushing down my cheeks into a torrent of unconditional love for myself and those I love. The warm, loving energy is around me as I lie on the soaked mattress. The gentle pressure of a full body embrace floods me with a magnified version of the same love and an unmistakable directive: "You are not heartbroken. You are soulbroken." The loving source whispered from inside of me: "Come back tomorrow."

---

*Traveler's Tip: Do Your Research*

I'm not suggesting that psychedelics are the answer to helping you heal your grief, but if they're of interest, I encourage you to learn more. You would be in good company: after a fifty-year ban, a team of researchers at Johns Hopkins University were recently permitted to resume the study of the therapeutic use of psychedelics in the United States, and has since launched the Center for Psychedelic and Consciousness Research. There, researchers will "use psychedelics to study the mind and identify therapies for diseases such as addiction, PTSD and Alzheimer's."[4]

---

## RECONCILING WITH RITUAL: BEGINNINGS

For me, three ayahuasca ceremonies were transformative in understanding myself and my grief. Among its many gifts, it answered old questions and raised new ones, too. Integrating back into my life at home, I began to wonder why there weren't more ceremonies and rituals for the experience of ambiguous grief—surely, plant medicine in foreign countries isn't the only conduit for healing! After a couple hours of searching, it was evident why there are no standard rituals marking ambiguous grief. Put simply: we ritualize our beginnings, not our endings.

This makes sense when we consider how endings are

"hard" and filled with those uncomfortable feelings most of us aren't well practiced in navigating. Just think about the last few parties you've attended or take a look at your own social media feed and you'll see what I mean. Not only do we celebrate our beginnings easily and often, we ensure they are well documented, too. Beginnings are captured by many people, from various angles and viewpoints, then edited with filters and enhanced with sound. All to ensure that our beginnings are post-worthy before immortalizing them for the masses via social media.

We celebrate our beginnings with familiar rituals immortalized in picture-perfect posts: candles adorn decadent birthday cakes, clinking champagne glasses on boomerang mode toast couples' engagements, pink- and blue-embellished gender-reveal parties excitedly announce "girl or boy," and public ribbon-cuttings declare the opening of new businesses. We celebrate our beginnings with words: singing the happy birthday song, reciting heartfelt poetry and generations-old wedding vows, and writing and reading speeches declaring our intent and thanking our supporters. We celebrate our beginnings with meaningful symbols: making a wish and blowing out our birthday candles, exchanging shiny rings as vows are proclaimed, and officially opening the red-bow-wrapped new business with oversized scissors.

These familiar rituals associated with our beginnings act as a rite of passage and mark the most monumental transitions in our lives. While such rituals often occur in the presence of an audience, it is not a requirement. For example, a person can celebrate their birthday alone, with the traditional elements of the birthday cake ritual, but without anyone else. Sure, it might sound a little sad or lonely, but it doesn't prevent the ritual from happening, and it can still be joyful. There's still cake, right? But when witnessed or shared, our ceremonies bestow the gifts of acknowledgment and validation, two treasures that allow us to reconcile our reality.

## Reconciling with Ritual: Endings

The most common and widely accepted ending ceremony is probably what we know as a funeral. In this ceremony, which honors the life of one who has died a physical death, there are many rituals. Family and friends gather, remembering the deceased with expressions of love, eulogizing their life with heartfelt stories, treasured photographs, and often food—lots of it. But what happens when we experience the loss of a relationship when our beloved is still living, or when one of those "beautiful beginnings" doesn't end as planned? While we may privately acknowledge the embarrassment of a failed business, the pain of a divorce, the isolation of cognitive decline, or the shame of an addiction, rarely do we do so publicly on the same social media platforms we used in celebration. It isn't because ending events aren't happening all around us; if we haven't had the experience ourselves, it's likely that we know someone who has. Yet our endings aren't advertised, so ambiguous grievers remain an underrepresented group.

I suspect that's because, unlike the beautiful "beginning" events that feature appealing emotions like excitement, joy, and pride, endings are often saddled with not-so-desirable emotions: sadness, failure, fear, embarrassment, and shame. On this, as researcher and storyteller Brené Brown explains in her book *Daring Greatly: How the Courage to Be Vulnerable Transforms the Way We Live, Love, Parent, and Lead*, "Shame is the most powerful, master emotion. It is the fear that we aren't good enough.... If you put shame in a Petri dish, it needs three ingredients to grow exponentially: secrecy, silence, and judgment. If you put the same amount of shame in a Petri dish and douse it with empathy, it can't survive."

No wonder ambiguous grievers aren't taking over social media feeds to put these hard, heavy, and uncomfortable emotions on display! But if we meet our endings in this way, with empathy instead of shame, perhaps we can change that. By embracing our own endings and tuning in to our grief, we begin to accept ourselves in a new way. Doing so can not only help you to better identify endings and honor the grief experience of those around you, but it may give permission for others to feel that they can do the same. In this way, grief becomes an agent that connects us to one another, uniting us in our shared humanity and reminding us, as psychologist and author Ram Dass once said, "We are all just walking each other home."

## EMBRACING YOUR ENDING

For Ilianna, regular attendance at Nar-Anon meetings gifted her with the understanding she'd been lacking. They helped her to reconcile that the man she loved was a good person, *and* the man she loved was addicted to narcotics. That her old life was gone, *and* that building a new life was in her power. As she shared with me: "The meetings were exactly what I needed to help me grieve and to accept my reality with help from repeating the 'Three C's'—I didn't cause it, I can't control it, and I can't cure it. Once I surrendered to that, I was open to looking at things differently. Specifically, I came to understand that I cannot be a fixer—it's just not possible—but I can be a helper. My job is to take care of me, and I did that by showing up at the meetings and working each step at my own pace."

After fifteen years of marriage and eight years of meetings, life in recovery is the new normal for Ilianna and Jim. "One day at a time," they are still together and each working their own recovery programs. The early feelings of shame are gone, and the pride in her voice is evident as she speaks of her husband. Her resentment has been replaced with admiration for his daily commitment to his recovery. Now, Ilianna no longer relies on false hope or the wrongly perceived notion that she can control others, and because the meetings were so instrumental in helping her to reconcile her reality, she continues to attend. "Recently," Ilianna said, "a newcomer asked me why I still keep coming to meetings. I told him that the program keeps me grounded and gives me the tools I need—but I also come to give *hope* to others, to show them there is a better way to live."

## CREATING A FAUX-U-NERAL

In the absence of structured meetings or a specific ceremony to recognize your loss, consider creating and implementing your own. In doing so, you begin to manufacture the very stepping-stones needed to build the **bridge of reconciliation**. You may find, as I did, that enacting a ritual or a ceremony to honor our endings is empathy in action—for ourselves and for one another. For instance, your ending ceremony may include memorializing your loss in a letter that you read aloud or reclaiming a momentous date by giving it new meaning. Perhaps you will honor your loss with a special trip or commemorative piece of art, clothing, or jewelry. For me, the concept of such an ending ritual was born from my experience in the jungle and manifested as what I came to call a *faux-u-neral*, a ceremony I created as a way to recognize the loss of my marriage. However, it can be used to celebrate and honor any ending that you're grieving.

It doesn't need to be a fancy event, so don't let cost or planning become an impediment. Mine was an intimate, simple lakeside ceremony with two dear friends who are more like family and knew my marriage well. We sat together on a blanket under the glow of the late afternoon sun with a beautiful blue heron standing nearby, an uninvited but welcome witness. As I eulogized my marriage, we cried with laughter in memory of what was, and we cried in sadness of what would not be. We cried together listening to the music playing from the makeshift rock altar that held my smartphone. I listened intently as I received the line of two mourners offering their sincere condolences. In this moment, my loss finally felt validated. I was seen not as a victim of someone else's choices or as a shell-shocked version of my former self, but, finally, as a wife who had lost her beloved husband. I had been a widow-in-waiting for over two years, abiding like an understudy in a role that I didn't know I needed to play. As we rose from the blanket by the shore, the uninvited guest rose, too. In a single swoop and with wings spread wide, the blue heron launched into the air, crossing in front of us before climbing higher and out of sight. As I watched the heron fly on, I recognized a deep knowing: that in honoring my ending and ritualizing my loss, I had readied my soulbroken self for flight.

---

### Exercise 16 | Plan a Faux-u-neral

Determine a time and place, invite others, prepare remarks, share photos, and select music meaningful to you or the relationship you're grieving. Whether in front of an audience of your two best friends, or you, your dog, and the moon, including another soul who can bear witness to your ritual is a powerful act that serves to validate the pain of an otherwise unceremonious loss. Share it on social media while you're at it, and perhaps together as we #honorendings, we can normalize loss, grow our collective empathy, and show others the value and beauty of grief.

Maybe someday, we will celebrate grief just as we do joy and create a culture where a beautiful bride, a weeping widow, and all ambiguous grievers are equally embraced and understood.

Invite others to shine a light on their endings, too. In doing so, you may just find:

- You aren't the only one who benefits from such a ceremony.
- Ambiguous grievers are more common than you may have thought.
- Faux-u-neral guests may be also be grieving the loss of the same person.

---

## CROSSING THE BRIDGE

Ceremonies and rituals help to honor the past and the present and reconcile complex, gnarly, and often contradictory emotions like love and pain, shame and pride, and regret and gratitude. They also offer added comfort and the benefits of social bonding, making our journey through ambiguous grief feel a little less lonely. Even more, I believe they are a pivotal tool that aids in integrating our opposing selves and reconciling your love and your loss.

Remember that reconciliation doesn't imply backward movement, but rather is accepting the relationship for what it once was and what it is now, even if that means acknowledging that there is no relationship. As you do this, however you decided to do it, you are moving yourself forward over the bridge and toward recovery. This is because, whether you pursue an ancient ceremony in the presence of a shaman or create your own ceremonial rituals in front of friends, the act of honoring your loss before others validates what was while concurrently accepting what is. In doing so, this act transforms your pain, converting it into a testament, not of your grief, but to your love. Not only because love is the original seed from which your grief grew, but because love is our universal language. In both life and death, it is love that connects us to each other as well as to our grief, and it is love that remains even long after our loved ones have gone. As you move into recovery, bring your love with you—you're going to need it.

## WISE WORDS ON RITUALS

"By participating in a ritual…you are being, as it were, put in accord with that wisdom, which is the wisdom that is inherent within you anyhow. Your consciousness is being re-minded of the wisdom of your own life."

—JOSEPH CAMPBELL

"The opposite of addiction isn't sobriety. It's connection.…It's all that will help [you], in the end. If you are alone, you cannot escape addiction. If you are loved, you have a chance. For a hundred years we have been singing war songs about addicts. All along, we should have been singing love songs to them."

—JOHANN HARI, *CHASING THE SCREAM: THE FIRST AND LAST DAYS OF THE WAR ON DRUGS*

"Ritual is the passageway of the soul into the infinite."

—ALGERNON BLACKWOOD

"You have to keep breaking your heart until it opens."

—RUMI

"The human soul can always use a new tradition. Sometimes we require them."

—PAT CONROY, *THE LORDS OF DISCIPLINE*

CHAPTER 6

# From Recovery to Regeneration

"I think your heart needs to be broken and broken
open at least once to have a heart at all or to have
a heart for others."

—RICHARD ROHR[1]

"What we once enjoyed and deeply loved we can
never lose, for all that we love deeply becomes a
part of us."

—HELEN KELLER

Since your activating event, you've battled your way through
grief's seemingly unrelenting campaign; you've freed yourself from the emotional roundabout, stopped the madness of
the hope cycle, walked the path of internal hope, and reconciled your way across a bridge you created, all for this—to get
here. Take a moment to be proud of yourself. You made it—as
you know, not everyone does, and not everyone chooses to
stay, either. Recovery is hard, especially in the beginning, and
it can be disappointing, too. Simply arriving at a hard-fought

destination doesn't instantly fulfill your desires, and it may even reveal more layers of reality for you to rethink. Beyond that, recovery isn't without obstacles; rather, it's littered with land mines—emotional explosives hidden under the surface that will require your navigational know-how to disarm.

## WHAT IS RECOVERY?

Over the years, recovery has been defined differently across organizations within the United States and around the globe. In recent years, the term has typically been associated with recovering from substance use disorders. In an effort to destigmatize addiction, the Recovery Research Institute, in its "Addictionary," defines recovery as "the process of improved physical, psychological, and social well-being and health after having suffered from a substance-related condition."[2] While this doesn't directly apply to recovery from various forms of grief, the sentiment does. Specific to grief, *The Grief Recovery Handbook* by John W. James and Russell Friedman defines recovery, in part, in the following ways: recovery is finding new meaning for living without the fear of being hurt again, being able to enjoy fond memories without having them turn painful, and acquiring the skills to help us deal with loss directly.[3]

For our purposes, recovery as it relates to ambiguous grief combines components of both. What helped me to really understand recovery wasn't someone else's definition, but rather determining my own. Instead of striving to live in a space of another's devising, I sought to construct it for myself. I started by reverse engineering the idea of what recovery is by first gaining clarity on what it isn't. While this may seem counterintuitive to you at first, think of yourself like the famous Renaissance artist Michelangelo, whose approach was similar. In creating his masterpiece *David*, Michelangelo is credited as saying, "The sculpture is already complete within the marble block before I start my work. It is already there; I just have to chisel away the superfluous material." By applying this rationale, you can create your own version of recovery by removing what it isn't to reveal what is. To me, recovery from ambiguous grief isn't:

- The same for everyone
- Achieved and then "done"
- A return to who you were before your loss

In deconstructing my three recovery "isn'ts," I ultimately revealed what this stage is for me and how to live forward. As you survey this space, be sure to take field notes; jotting down your "isn'ts" as you find them will ultimately help you to define what recovery is for you. When I admitted that my lifelong physical activity of choice, running, no longer served me as it once had, that small acknowledgment of what my recovery didn't look like made space for what it does look like, and a love for hiking was born. Your discoveries may not be what you expect, but try to stay open to your observations. Recovery itself is a process, and so, too, is defining and shaping it for yourself. As you chip away at what it isn't, you'll slowly transition into the life that you've created for yourself. Just keep your eyes on your own path, respecting without judgment that what others need may not be helpful for you, and vice versa. As you enter and begin to get acquainted with this final stage, I recommend arming yourself with the tool of love, especially in the beginning, because recovery isn't the same for everyone, and neither are transitions.

## TWO STORIES ABOUT RECOVERY

In order to better understand recovery, we'll look at it from a couple of different angles. Similar to looking at a piece of art, perspective can influence your interpretation and even shape your experience. Even still, both art and recovery are subjective; two people can view a portrait from the same vantage point and still experience it differently. Vicki, a parent grieving for a child's old gender identity, and Alex, a man who accepted his own new one, both struggled with ambiguous grief brought on by the same activating event. While their stories represent different perspectives, each is grounded in love, loss, and a deep desire for validation. Though their time spent in recovery differs, both found the transition to this stage to be a challenge.

## Not the Same for Everyone

"It's been really difficult, but it was worse in the beginning," Vicki said, recounting her experience with ambiguous grief. "When my adult daughter sat me down and told me to start using the pronouns 'they/them,' I felt confused. I didn't understand, but I tried. Soon after, at another sit-down, they let me know about scheduling a surgery to transition to male, and that's when I went numb. I sobbed. I was overwhelmed with grief and would cry all the time, even at work. Some days I was angry or in a state of denial. Bargaining was especially prevalent early on. I spent a lot of my time saying plenty of 'foxhole' prayers—you know, if God does *x*, I will do *y*. I was so desperate not to lose my child. I know my child wasn't dying a physical death like we think of it, but it felt like it, in many ways. I love my child no matter what. What hurts is that I never felt that I was validated in my grief."

For many parents in Vicki's position, navigating the unprecedented experience of a child's transitioning can feel confusing and may prove an overwhelming experience fraught with complicated and conflicting feelings. It is often an alienating experience as well, with parents not sharing about the transition for different reasons. It may be requested of the parent that they not share with others, or perhaps the parent makes the decision not to share. Regardless of the reason, if the parent doesn't seek emotional support somewhere, they may find themselves in isolation and unable to support their own needs, much less be of support to the child they love. Just weeks after her child's disclosure, Vicki found herself alone and fearful, but not for reasons she expected. Though she had not spoken to anyone about it, honoring her adult child's wishes to not share with friends or family members, she was at risk of losing the relationship with her child anyway. This was because, as she says, "I wasn't allowed to make mistakes and I wasn't allowed to grieve, and, of course, I did both.

"What's really hard is that they were all honest mistakes, like use of their 'dead name,' which was perceived as 'transphobic.' I am not transphobic, and neither are those in my parental support group. The truth is that we are parents who are also in a transition of our own; saying goodbye to the person we raised, to our relationship, and to all the dreams we had. If I use their 'dead name,' it's not because I'm transphobic or unsupportive, it's because I've been using that name for decades. I chose that name with great love; I've been using that name for them since before they took their first breath. I will call my child by whatever name they prefer, because I love my child. I don't love their gender or an absence of gender. I love their soul."

## Acting the Part

Understandably, there's need for compassion for all who are trying to process and adapt to familial changes, both the individual transitioning and those around them. As Vicki's story hinted, individuals who are transitioning are often rejected by family members in varying degrees after announcing their truth. This was the case with Alex, another ambiguous griever I met who transitioned genders ten years ago. Alex told me: "It was so hard to be told by my own parents that there was something wrong with me, that in honoring who I felt I really was, I could no longer be a part of the family that I loved. My parents and extended family live in the area, which has made life, especially holidays, really hard, especially in the beginning.

"It's better for me now, but at first, it was so painful; seeing their cars outside my childhood home was so upsetting. I knew everyone was gathering inside to take part in all of the beloved traditions I enjoyed growing up, and, knowing them, they were all talking about how much I've hurt everyone. I really hoped that just one of them would speak up for me and help the others to see me as the me I've always been. I'm just now in a body that looks more like it was always supposed to. I had been told that I could attend, but only as long as I showed up as the person they wanted to see, as the person they knew me to be. But I couldn't act anymore—I had acted for so long in a body that never felt like it was mine. I finally didn't have to act anymore and was beyond disappointed that not one of them could even try to act happy for me. They just disowned me."

Unwilling to play the role required to be accepted back with family, Alex has spent the better part of the last decade working through ambiguous grief and finding ways to heal and live a new, happy life. Ultimately, we must accept that longing for loved ones who are unable to love us, for whatever reason, doesn't help us to heal, but learning to love differently can. Whether it's outspoken or silent, loud or quiet, in person or from afar, love is something you can summon as needed and use as you continue on your path.

## Academy Awards

As both stories show us, experiencing the change of a loved one's gender identity can come with a steep learning curve and is something worthy of compassion for all involved. Though they aren't related, both Vicki and Alex represent a parent/child relationship with the same activating event, and I found it interesting that both mentioned acting as a component in their experience. "I should get an Oscar for my performance," Vicki chuckled. "I'm acting my way through this right now. Each interaction follows the carefully outlined 'script' they gave me detailing what I can and cannot say.

"The narrative from within the trans community is that 'the trans community is to be celebrated,' and I agree with that. I love my child; I want to celebrate my child. This narrative also leaves no room for acknowledging the grief parents and close family members may feel. For all the talk about compassion, there's none I've felt toward myself or seen for parents on the receiving end of this news. There is no talk of compassion for us—it's as though our expressing our grief isn't permitted, not if we want to maintain a relationship, anyway."

"I finally found My People through a group I never would have expected," Vicki told me: "Evangelical Christian parents of LGBTQ people who stuck with their kids and were kicked out of their churches for it. Their losses vary, but most are… grieving the loss of their marriages, friends, family, or even their job. They have welcomed some parents of nonbinary and trans grievers like me into their group, and although it's not the exact same, it's as close as we can find right now for helping me figure out what this 'new normal' looks like and how to navigate through it. I didn't want to stay stuck in grief forever, and I didn't want my child to cut me out of their life, so this is how I'm finding my way forward. If I have to 'act' for my child like I'm not sometimes grieving, then that's what I'll do. When I need to, I can bring my grief to my group, where it's allowed."

Both Vicki and Alex experienced ambiguous grief from the same activating event but from different vantage points. Though the roles are different for each of them, both are navigating recovery in different ways; for Alex, it's a resolve not to "act" anymore and to focus on those who are accepting without requirement or condition. For Vicki, it's finding joy in the presence of her child even if doing so requires her to rehearse her stage notes before each visit, fearing she'll be cut from the script if she delivers the wrong line. However, one noteworthy commonality stands out as the tool of choice for both as they live in recovery from grief: love.

## *Love Is a Tool*

For both, love is the tool they are honing as they begin to live forward, finally at peace in accepting that their relationships are no longer what they once were and are now redefined under a different set of rules. But because love is also malleable, it is the perfect tool for ambiguous grievers to call upon, especially during this part of the journey. You may have noticed its subtle appearance in Alex's story or in John's, the father you met in Chapter 1. Though one is a son estranged from his family and the other is a father estranged from his daughter, both have resolved to leverage the tool of love from afar; in silent memories, quiet prayers, and newly formed rituals.

Conversely, you can adapt your love to a form suited for in-person interactions as well. We saw this in Beth, as she transitioned her mother into a memory care facility, choosing her actions out of love, a fountain from which kindness, tenderness, and dignity could flow. Vicki modeled this as well, finding that love has been a tool that sustains her, one that she can use when needed, as needed. Her self-professed "award-winning performances" may appear disingenuous at first glance, but through the lens of love, we see a mother not wanting to lose a relationship she treasures any more than she feels she already has.

In this way, Vicki is applying a concept of emotion that we touched on in Chapter 4. The "acting as if" principle is built on the work of nineteenth-century psychologist William James, who believed that our actions guide our emotions, not the other way around (e.g., we laugh and so we feel happy, not we feel happy, so we laugh). Recent work on the idea supports the concept that conscious and intentional behavior can positively influence a desired behavioral outcome. *The As-If Principle* by Richard Wiseman offers examples, such as nodding as you speak if you want to be more persuasive, eating with your nondominant hand if you want to lose weight, or acting like a newlywed if you want to rekindle romance with your partner.

Whether or not Vicki is knowingly applying the "as-if" principle, her desired outcome is rooted in love. So, for now, she acts her way through their in-person interactions and tells me this isn't uncommon for parents having a similar experience. "We come from all different backgrounds, but are bound by our unique loss and our decision not to reject or abandon our children," she told me. "I think this illustrates a powerful truth about my new community of trans and nonbinary parents: it doesn't matter our socioeconomic, cultural, or religious affiliation—across it all, parents who are trying to understand their transitioning or transitioned child want to learn because we love our children. Love is the center of it all, and we love our children no matter what their gender was or is. I always have and I always will."

---

## Love Warning Label

This tool is not intended for all experiencing ambiguous grief and may not be suitable for the following travelers:

- Those whose loss involved trauma
- Those who experience PTSD
- Those who have not yet fully experienced the emotions and feelings associated with the stages of grief
- Those who are not actively practicing internal hope or able to identify external hope and cycling

Discontinue use of this tool if it causes onset of languishing, longing, or other signs of extended grief or complicated or prolonged grief disorder.

---

## Exercise 17 | Love Memories

Take a moment to recall the love you have for the person you are grieving. If your circumstances are such that another emotion, like anger, may be making it difficult for you to feel love for that person, think about a time when your love was intact. Allow your memory to travel to the moments when love was shared between you. Can you remember three of them? Write them down in as much detail as you can recall.

For example, one of my love memories is set on my honeymoon. For the first two days, we walked for hours and miles touring the new-to-us city together, visiting museums, attractions, and restaurants. By the third day, we were exhausted but still wanted to explore. We found a green double-decker tour bus the most desirable way to continue our sightseeing. Even though we were by far the youngest passengers aboard, we rode the bus all day, leaving our upper-deck seats only to go down the stairs and buy tickets to keep those seats on the next tour.

Recalling these love memories and writing them out allows you to remember the love and hone it as a tool in your healing. The more you reflect on your love memories, the more detail you may uncover, too. Tap into the senses that each memory carries for you: sight, smell, taste, touch, and sound. As you do, be sure to edit the written version of your love memory to include the remembered details. Once it's fully formed, allow yourself to tap into the memory, the emotion of it all, and specifically the love you felt in those moments. As you feel yourself feeling that love, imagine yourself bottling the sensations and keeping them as tools—you'll likely be using them frequently.

When you step on a land mine of grief, as you sometimes will, and find yourself feeling overwhelmed and cycling, reach for your love memories. Get quiet and call them through the ether to you; let them flood through you; allow yourself to feel that love and imagine sending it to the person you're grieving. In whatever way you decide to sit with and send your love, you may ultimately find, as I did, that love is a powerful tool for quelling the erratic waves of grief that arise throughout this phase of your journey.

For some, however, this does not apply. This is because not all loves are left intact when loss occurs. While love is often preserved when we endure the physical death of our loved one, that isn't always the case for those whose loved ones go on living, thereby allowing for additional interaction, hurt, and harm. For these soulbroken travelers, and for losses involving trauma, calling upon love may prove more harmful than helpful. Be sure to read the warning label and talk it over with your own Amy to determine if it's a tool that is right for you.

---

---

## Land Mines

Even though you have worked so hard to get to a place of recovery, the pain of your loss isn't something that you could outwork or outrun. No one can. Pain born from a soulbreak doesn't dissipate—it assimilates, becoming part of you. It will be with you throughout this stage and will be with you beyond here. This might be hard to understand at first, but the work you've done to heal was never meant to erase your loss or your pain, but rather to help you get acquainted with it so you can learn to manage this part of you and integrate it into your life. In the way one may manage a chronic health condition like migraines or diabetes, whenever you feel the current of your ambiguous grief stirring, you can rely on everything you've learned throughout your journey to help anchor yourself so you don't get carried off by rough waters.

Let's start by mapping out your potential minefields, those that you can easily identify and therefore navigate preemptively. Start with those that you can know, like dates on the calendar. Holidays and anniversaries are often fertile ground for explosives: since they are filled with memories and traditions from the past, they can easily trigger grief and draw out depression or activate anger. Since there's no stopping time, you can't avoid them and can count on confronting these dates year after year. However, you do have the capacity to reframe these land mines and manage the force of their impact by preparing for them in advance by identifying all potential dates, locations, events, and other associations that dredge up painful reminders of your loss and devising an alternate plan. One way I do this is by getting out of town on specific dates, opting instead to spend time hiking in nature instead of sitting in my home, a place that, on these days, feels like returning to the scene of the crime. There are certain events and outings I find especially triggering; for these, I give myself permission to show up in whatever way I need to, whether it means staying for ten minutes instead of an hour or not attending at all. Put simply, I am committed to traversing events in whatever ways take the very best care of me.

Of course, not all land mines can be sidestepped, so you should prepare yourself for inevitable detonations. They may hit you from seemingly innocuous sources: the scent of your loved one's perfume on a stranger passing by, their favorite song playing as you shop for groceries—such invasions of our senses have the power to sideswipe and stun, especially if triggered without warning. For such surprise attacks, remember to reach for the tools to help you regain your footing. Meditate, practice mindfulness, sort and file what you can control, or reread your rules of disengagement. Those, along with the final tools I'm about to share, work well in such instances. Just remember that land mines, like recovery itself, will look different for everyone, and your experience of this stage may not be the same as for others, but that doesn't make anyone right or wrong.

---

## RECOVERY ISN'T FIXED

Just as experiences of grief stages aren't neat or linear, neither is recovery. While recovery isn't the same for everyone, those in recovery understand a universal truth: recovery isn't something "achieved" and then "completed" like conquering some sort of video game and never considering it again. While it's true that we have been pursuing this place throughout our travels, arriving here in recovery doesn't mean that we have crossed an imaginary finish line and can now prop up our tired feet and bask in the glow of our new, easy lives. Arriving here is more of a bookend to our journey—it was never the goal and for most of us, it isn't the end. Fortunately (or unfortunately depending on your viewpoint), recovery offers more than just a respite after your woeful journey. It also presents you with an array of new opportunities that will invite you to challenge yourself and consider yourself and your world differently. That's because these new thoughts are born from the experience of your journey. Just as your love and your loss are unique to you, so, too, is how you've traveled your path and the learning you've gathered along the way. Before going on, take a few moments to reflect on the wisdom you've gained with the following prompt.

---

*Exercise 18 | Good Things Happen in Threes*

Consider completing the sentence "During my time grieving, I have learned _____." Begin with three items at a minimum, but don't censor yourself—write out as many as you are able. We'll circle back to these in our final debrief.

---

As you reflect on what you've learned so far through this experience, you will likely see that the capacity for growth doesn't end simply because you've arrived in recovery. The reality is that living in recovery affords us lifelong learning in the form of thousands of unique lessons. Whether you have endured a broken leg, a substance use disorder, or ambiguous grief, recovering takes more than just time—it takes focused and sustained effort. While time passes, we can choose to say "yes" to the new opportunities we encounter and, in doing so, continue to learn and grow. Reading a book, making a friend, and trying acupuncture are all examples that you can choose to explore, but whose gifts can only be realized after actualizing the opportunity. Balancing an open mind with your own discernment is key, since you know better than anyone what healing modalities and hobbies excite you and which don't. Even if you try something and don't like it, and you learn that you "never want to do that again," that's okay, because learning that is also a gift (aerial yoga, I'm looking at you).

Whether you find your new experiences to be enjoyable or not, energy is required to both engage in and later process the activity. If you sometimes feel weary, almost weighted down by your learning, you are equipped for the task of recovery! If you are weary even without an accumulation of learning and you really just want to sit and cry awhile, then you may have skipped ahead on the path or taken a wrong turn somewhere, and should probably retrace your steps until you're back in the right spot. You'll find your way here when you're ready, but you really do need to do the work first. You might be able to shortcut yourself into this stage, but you won't be able to stick around very long, because you simply can't hack your way into healing. Members of AA know this: recovery is a safe place to set up camp, but only after you have honestly found your way through.

## Recovery Roster

The transition into recovery is smoother when you have others around you who understand the landscape. These may be people you already know, or you may find them only once you've arrived. However you find them, just be sure that you do. Staying connected to Your People, whether in the form of virtual or in-person support groups, can be wildly helpful early on in your grief.

At this stage of your healing, however, it's likely you're not relying on Your People as much as you once did. As you expand your activities and engage more with others, think of them as your "Special Ops" team: you've been bonded by battle and can call on them as reinforcements when needed. But as you adjust to your new life in recovery, it's helpful to review who and what you have in your general company. An intentional way to do so is to create your Recovery Roster—a list of the people, groups, and events with whom you engage regularly. The purpose of this roster is twofold: to help you consciously consider how you spend your time, and how those engagements impact your grief. For example, if you're recovering from the loss of your best friend due to estrangement, dinner with mutual friends may trigger you back to external hope. If these mutual friends overlap as Your People, boundaries established in advance can act as guardrails to help keep your conversation from going off-course and crashing head-on into external hope. The same is true no matter your activating event. For instance, if you're now grieving the loss of your mother to mental illness, your long-standing role chairing the local Mother's Day luncheon may not be in your best interest.

As you give your roster thoughtful consideration, think about who you want around you in the new space you are creating for yourself. For example, though you may enjoy those mutual friends or your position on the event committee, they may not serve your emotional well-being, at least not at this time. Regardless of association with your loved one, there's an infinite number of reasons you may determine some currently on your roster are no longer a good fit. While they don't necessarily need to be additive to your healing, they definitely cannot be something that hinders it. Sometimes deciphering between the two can be tricky, but an easy test may help you gauge the difference: simply notice how you feel when you leave their company. Are you uplifted and energized, or drained and discouraged? If the latter is the norm, it may be time to assess their place on your roster. Another way to determine who is a good fit is to make a list of the top ten characteristics and attributes you value. You can use this list to qualify potential candidates as well as rethink existing ones. It doesn't mean those who don't make the cut can't be part of your life, but it does offer you a quick reference list to cross-check. Doing so can help to illuminate which members of your roster to retain, recruit, or release.

As you become more acquainted with what and who is best for your healing, it's likely you'll also realize who is not.

While this can be difficult, releasing what no longer serves you is a normal part of life, especially as you acclimate to this stage. Give yourself permission to let go, and if you need assistance, review the tools you picked up in Chapter 4 and use them again. Even as you become comfortable here, you may still find occasions where you need to dust off those tools not only to let go of your loved one (again), but to release others as well. Be gentle with yourself when this happens. Remember that letting go is a process and rarely realized on the first try. Whether it's one or a hundred times, practicing letting go is what is needed in order to firmly anchor yourself in acceptance. Once you do, the gifts of this stage begin to emerge more clearly.

## THE HERO'S JOURNEY

For some, the idea of recovery indicates a return to what was "before"; before the injury, the substance abuse, the loss. But recovery from what ails us doesn't always mean a return to being as we once were—healed, sober, or joyful. It's no wonder we should suppose this; after all, the concept is pervasive in our entertainment—from childhood books to classic live-action and animated pictures, audiences love characters on a quest, overcoming obstacles and villains, complete with a tidy, enlightening ending. We are relieved when our hero returns triumphant and resumes life in a full-circle sequence, like Dorothy waking up in Kansas with friends and family at her bedside. This plot structure deeply resonates within us and is one seemingly woven into our DNA. From ancient mythological stories to modern day screenwriting, we witness our stories' heroes as they're called to an adventure, receive supernatural aid, meet mentors, face challenges and temptations, fail, transform, and return.

Joseph Campbell, author of the 1949 book *The Hero with a Thousand Faces*, is credited with first recognizing this plot pattern as recurrent in human storytelling and naming it "the hero's journey." Though Campbell indicates that the hero returns with the gifts born from the difficult journey, I believe this doesn't mark the end of the experience. Rather, the end is marked in a few different ways, including in how we do or do not recognize those gifts we've accrued, and more importantly, what it is we do with them. Whether it's Dorothy's desire to return home or yours to return to your pre-loss self, it's hard to imagine either of you would simply be able to resume life as it once was. After all, how could you, knowing all that you know now? You've been tested, you've overcome, you've learned, and if you've been open to the process along the way and worked through real-world exercises and those in this book, then you've likely also grown. If so, it means that you are emerging into this season with new perspectives: on life, love, loss, grief, yourself, and more. This is a component of our grief stories that, too often, we fail to unearth. In doing so, we neglect to discover our own treasure, and if we don't do that, it cannot be of service to ourselves or others. That is why recovery isn't a return to your old self, and why you shouldn't want it to be.

# MEANING

There's a certain phenomenon I noticed occurring within myself as I began to examine the ambiguous grief process. I went back to my data looking for breadcrumbs that might indicate a common denominator among those who were, in Amy's words, "living life on the other side." What I suspected was confirmed nearly in real time, when grief expert David Kessler released his work revealing meaning as the sixth stage of grief. It's also the next-to-last tool for your journey, so let's explore what meaning means and where you may find yours.

If you're rolling your eyes right now, I don't blame you. Depending on your unique experience with loss, grief, and healing, you may have zero interest in learning about meaning. You may assume that meaning is just as incorrigible as the other stages in the group, because birds of a feather fly together, right? I get it, because we know that the original stages of grief (denial, bargaining, anger, depression, and acceptance) are unpleasant, mangy houseguests that come and go as they please. But not meaning. I like to think of meaning as the only houseguest among the group who's actually been invited, the one who respects boundaries and shows up only when asked. Sure, I've noticed meaning passing by on occasion, but as the well-mannered stage that it is, meaning waits for a proper invitation. However, navigating this stage and honing it as a tool are not without challenges—namely, determining the right time to extend the invitation and recalling it swiftly when or if you need to.

## Meeting Meaning

Like most wise teachers, meaning doesn't deliver you from your troubles by giving you the answers you want or by telling you what your path should or shouldn't entail. Instead, meaning patiently listens and reflects your own wisdom back to you. Meaning may know the answer, but it doesn't share it, knowing that you must discover the answer for yourself. You have to listen closely to intuit the answer inside you, but meaning will affirm you when you do. In a way, meaning is the Amy among the mangy houseguests, and while not a mandatory tool for healing, it's a potentially influential one—but only when you are ready.

In *Finding Meaning: The Sixth Stage of Grief,* David Kessler writes that "the first step in finding meaning is the fifth stage of grief: acceptance."[4] While this was intended for those grieving loved ones who have died a physical death, it applies nicely to us ambiguous grievers as well. Whether we are experiencing grief from physical death or ambiguous grief from an activating event, if we have been unable to accept the reality of our loss, then attempts to connect meaning to that loss will be futile. This is because meaning is anchored in acceptance, and, like a rope you use to climb up a mountain, it's only as sturdy as the rock that anchors it. While the strands of meaning can quickly braid together to form a reliable rope, it will break easily if acceptance is not as sturdy as it needs to be. And, like all rocks that make up great mountains, acceptance has to undergo a long, slow process of formation, taking its shape by enduring each season of pain time and again.

Though duration varies, the ambiguous grievers I interviewed indicated an average period of four years before they felt they'd fully experienced acceptance. So be sure to give yourself grace if you're not there yet. Remember, acceptance isn't apathy or approval, it's acknowledgment that what is, is, without sustained desire or longing for it to be anything else. When you notice that you aren't needing to let go as often as you once did, that your time spent languishing in longing has sizably shortened, or that your desire for what "was" has become but a fleeting thought or nicety you're able to dismiss, then it may be time.

You may have interacted with meaning at various points along your path, but if you attempted to tackle this mountain before your rope was anchored and your rock was ready, then odds are you didn't make it very far. Or perhaps you started climbing and discovered you weren't quite ready to charge the summit. For me, that happened when I started sharing about my grief in online articles and attached my meaning to the idea of helping others wrestling with ambiguous grief. But as I began hearing back from those others, I found myself overwhelmed, and aspects of my own grief were triggered. As much as I wanted to find meaning, the way I'd gone about it diverted me from the path I'd been on and turned a modest hill into an insurmountable mountain. I let go of the rope and returned to the place on my path where I'd left off, and in doing so, I also allowed the pain of each passing season to push my rock deep into the earth, where it still remains, firmly grounded.

## Right Rope, Wrong Time

While I wasn't wrong—writing and sharing my learning openly with others is how I've found my meaning—I couldn't have been more wrong in my timing—I grabbed onto my meaning and took off for the summit far too soon. Maybe that came out of my own desperation to make sense of my loss, or perhaps having my truth witnessed and validated was such a needed and natural feel-good hit of serotonin that I held on. Whatever it was, it was premature. So, know that it's always okay to drop the rope when you realize the time for meaning just isn't right. When you're ready, you'll know it and can try again. When you do, your meaning may be the same as when you left it, or it may present in a different form entirely, having diverged or evolved into something else.

## When Meaning Isn't Applicable

The concept itself may feel contrived or pointless, especially if your loss was incurred in a traumatic way or is so soulbreaking that you simply can't imagine ascribing any meaning worthy of your great loss. Meaning is manmade, conceived to try to form sense around those things we otherwise cannot. Some losses are so profoundly unfair, unjust, and pointless that assigning them a measly meaning feels as pointless and nonsensical as the loss you've endured—a freak accident that left your once-healthy child unable to communicate, or the untreated mental illness of your once-doting father, whose multiple tours of duty have since haunted him into homelessness. For some, looking for meaning can feel like a trite effort to assuage tragedy.

If you know this level of soulbreak, and meaning is just one more thing heaped onto the pile of a growing number of things that don't make sense, you're under no obligation to make meaning of anything just now. Even if your acceptance is solid, you aren't required to search for meaning. If you feel this way, you don't need to be polite about it, either, so own it: "I see you, Meaning. But I'm not interested." Slam the door on meaning if you need to—it is abundantly okay. Because of all the lousy character traits the gang of mangy grief houseguests have between them, meaning has a quality that damn near redeems them all: meaning is deferential. This stage is patient and will wait outside until *you* welcome it in. Meaning respects your timing, your loss, and your grief. But probably the greatest gift of meaning is its ability to help you drop the hot potato. As meaning moves in, you'll notice, in time, that you're no longer suffering as you once were. Because like empathy to shame, meaning smothers suffering; neither pair can coexist.

While meaning isn't a panacea for the pain of your soul-breaking loss, no one thing is. But like all forms of pain management, it does provide relief, alleviating the intensity of your pain and reducing the swelling around your soul. Even if you're still pretty certain that meaning isn't for you, I invite you to be willing to check in on it now and again. When you feel meaning might be lurking around, consider your options and remember that, like a loyal friend or steadfast therapist, meaning will be there for you when you decide to reach out.

## RECOVERY RECAP

When remembering the start of your journey and the difficult days that surrounded your activating event, it may feel impossible to have imagined you'd one day arrive in a space such as this. Take a quick inventory—see, you survived. More than that, you're actually okay. You may even be experiencing positive feelings that have escaped you for a long time. Together, we've navigated a gnarled and nuanced landscape, and whether you pushed yourself on every exercise or half-assed them all, the journey was demanding. As our time together nears its end, I'm not going to grab my pom-poms and fill you with euphemisms like "It all happened for a reason," "It was all worth it," or "It didn't happen to you, it happened for you," because I just don't believe those to be helpful. What I do believe is that the loss you've endured has caused you great pain, and the only reason you met this great grief is because you also met its counterpart, great love. I don't know why it happened or what meaning you'll find in it, if any; that's up to you. But I do know that it's impossible to undergo a loss such as this without it changing you on some level. As you continue to evolve in recovery, I encourage you to keep love and meaning close at hand. The more you use them, the more you are allowing the fullest and brightest Technicolor version of yourself to take shape.

From my own vantage point in recovery, I now see that my life is colored with diverse and immeasurable gifts that I didn't have prior to my activating event. I'm connected more deeply to myself, my higher power, and my loved ones. I've added enriching insights, experiences, and relationships that I wouldn't otherwise have had and couldn't have imagined for myself back then. As I deconstructed what recovery wasn't and started to construct what it was, I realized it wasn't what I thought it would be. Perhaps the word itself misled me into thinking I was traveling a full-circle route, one that would return me to my initial state prior to the cyclone of my activating event. After all, the most common definitions of what it means to recover are built on the concept of "returning to" something. As described in the *Oxford English Dictionary*, the origin of the word "recover" itself gave me pause: "re-," a prefix derived from Latin meaning "again, back"; and "cover" from mid-twelfth-century Old French "covrir," meaning "to cover, hide, and conceal," and Old English "covert," meaning "not openly acknowledged, displayed or avowed." In deconstructing the word, I viewed its literal interpretation to mean that to recover and live in a place of recovery is not something to be proud of, but rather an action to cover, conceal, and deny the something that brought me here—in my case, my loss and my grief. But with my world now in Technicolor, that's a big ask; I didn't want to disavow the emotional, physical, and spiritual turmoil, and all I had endured and learned.

Even though I had barely arrived, I started to believe a word that more aptly describes my emotional landscape is *regeneration*. As defined by Merriam-Webster, to regenerate is to be formed or created again; spiritually reborn; restored to a better, higher, or more worthy state; to change radically, and for the better. In viewing "recovery" from a different angle, I found within it an implied striving to hide and conceal what has pained you and return to where you once were, as who you once were. In regeneration, I interpret the intention as more affirming. For me, it reads as an invitation to strive to embrace and honor what has been painful, and, like the natural condition that is grief itself, to use that experience and its gifts for my rebirth.

From whatever angle you are viewing recovery and with whatever word best describes this space for you, I hope you will spend time here to reflect on how your awful, amazing, ridiculous, unfair, confusing (insert your own adjective here) journey has changed you, even if it's not necessarily a change for the better. As you reflect and rethink this stage and what it means for you, you may find that perhaps healing happens more naturally when you are not trying to recover anything, especially your grief. Instead, when you choose to leave your grief open and exposed to life, you actually begin to unfold to it naturally, like a flower to the sun. In doing so, you'll find that the grief you once sought to bury is now not only a part of you but is a vital component of your recovery, a springboard that is launching you into a leveled-up version of yourself.

Your space for recovery is unique to you and your experience. It's an ongoing process that requires effort and intentional choice, and it's an opportunity to experience life in a new, more vibrant way by being brave enough to examine what you've learned about yourself along the way. You may be surprised at what you find.

## WISE WORDS ON LOVE AND MEANING

"All that is real in our past is the love we gave and the love we received."
—MARIANNE WILLIAMSON, *A RETURN TO LOVE*

"In some ways suffering ceases to be suffering at the moment it finds a meaning, such as the meaning of a sacrifice."
—VIKTOR FRANKL

"Love is like quicksilver in the hand. Leave the fingers open and it stays. Clutch it, and it darts away."
—DOROTHY PARKER

"Love is patient, love is kind; love does not envy or boast; it is not arrogant or rude. It does not insist on its own way; it is not irritable or resentful; it does not rejoice at wrongdoing, but rejoices with the truth. Love bears all things, believes all things, hopes all things, endures all things. Love never ends."
—THE BIBLE, 1 CORINTHIANS 13:4–8

## CHAPTER 7

# The *Other* F Word and Life on the Other Side

"Listen. Slide the weight from your shoulders and
move forward. You are afraid you might forget, but
you never will. You will forgive and remember."
—BARBARA KINGSOLVER, *THE POISONWOOD
BIBLE*

Though our time together is nearly finished, we have one
more stop to explore before starting to unpack. This leg of
our journey examines forgiveness, an aspect of the grief process that many ambiguous grievers encounter. Depending on
a variety of aspects unique to you and your grief, the amount
of effort you put in here will vary. For some, it will be easy
and require little to no exertion, but for others it will be a slog
and require all the emotional energy you have left. Whatever
it may feel like for you now, I recommend setting an intention before you proceed. Whether your intention is to learn
as much as possible or just to get through it, remember to go

at your own pace and pause at any time. To help you prepare for what's ahead, take a moment to review the points of interest we'll be exploring:

- What forgiveness is for you and why
- Whether forgiveness is relevant to your grief
- Allowing forgiveness to find you
- Apologies as a vehicle for forgiveness
- Absent apologies
- Forgiving, forgetting, both, or neither
- Life on the other side

Along the way, we'll look at forgiveness from several different perspectives and dig deeper with one emotionally intensive exercise. But to begin, I invite you to consider a simple children's story, from the collection *Aesop's Fables*. Aesop's stories have informed readers of all ages for over two thousand years and are still shared around the world today. Two of his most well-known works continue to stand the test of time: "The Tortoise and The Hare," which teaches new readers that arrogance can be defeated by persistence, and "The Wolf in Sheep's Clothing," through which we learn that appearances can be deceiving. While not as popular, "The Man and the Serpent" is another of Aesop's fables. It's about forgiveness, and we'll use it to guide us as we go. Take a deep breath, set your intention, and begin when you're ready.

There was once a boy who was out playing on his father's farm when he accidently stepped on a snake, who in turn bit him, and the boy died. Filled with rage, the boy's father set off with his axe to find the snake. When he found it, the man cut off its tail. In response, the snake took revenge by biting the man's cattle herd, which caused the man great loss. The man then decided to try to make peace with the snake. He brought an offering of honey to the snake's nest and suggested that they agree to forgive and forget, reasoning that perhaps the snake was right in its actions, as he was surely right in his own, so they could call it even. The snake rejected him and told him to take the gifts away: It couldn't forget the loss of its tail any more than the man could forget the loss of his son.

Though this fable adapted over time, the original lesson about forgiving and forgetting has remained: some injuries can be forgiven but not forgotten, especially within the presence of the one who has harmed you. Perhaps that's why this particular fable isn't as well known. It's not that Aesop's insight is antiquated, but, as you'll soon discover, it doesn't neatly conform to the Western world's modern-day narrative of forgiveness.

If you're not sure what you believe about forgiveness or how it may even be relevant to your grief, you aren't alone. With over 2,500 studies and counting, researchers have yet to reach a consensus on the definition of forgiveness, much less qualify the process or quantify the benefits (or lack thereof). Current research on forgiveness offer several theories, among them:

- Forgiveness is a motivational, social instinct that evolved alongside revenge and solved problems for ancestral humans. (Michael McCollough)[1]
- Forgiveness is a decision based on willpower and "letting go" of resentment and bitterness. (DiBlasio)[2]
- Forgiveness occurs through changes in how one thinks of the transgression and transgressor, transforming the thoughts from negative to neutral or positive. (Laura Thompson, et al.)[3]
- Forgiveness is an act that occurs as a person moves out of emotions such as anger, resentment, and vengefulness and moves toward empathy, compassion, and altruistic love. (Everett Worthington)[4]
- Forgiveness is a choice but in order to fully forgive, a willing individual must choose to work through a process and make cognitive, affective, and behavioral changes. (Robert Enright)[5]

Regardless of how it happens, the general consensus is that forgiveness can be initiated in various ways as a result of many different changes, including a willful decision, behavior of the trangressor, or a defining emotional or spiritual experience. Additional consensus is that there are more positive outcomes from forgiveness than negative, including improvement of physical and mental health. All the more reason to want to find forgiveness, right?

Unfortunately, forgiveness isn't easy, and many ambiguous grievers may never experience it. That's not because we are a resentful, angry bunch, but because forgiveness is complex and influenced by many highly personal variables. Since I'm far from an expert on "the other F word," our focus will center on how it may relate to your ambiguous grief experience. To do this, let's look at a phenomenon I call "faux-giveness," a perspective familiar to many grieving the loss of a loved one still living.

## A FALSE START

Early in my own grief, I was startled to find the topic of forgiveness broached to me by others. Their comments ranged from thinly veiled inquiries to earnest imploring that increased in frequency as time passed. While I was battling my way through grief's assault, a handful of well-meaning supporters launched an interrogation campaign. While I would respectfully try to explain that my relationship with forgiveness was different than theirs, few accepted that. Some became defensive or disappointed, and I'd leave the conversation feeling that I'd somehow let them down. While this was curious to me at the time, I soon understood why it was happening and that I wasn't alone. Ambiguous grievers are often encouraged to forgive early and often—a partner who betrayed them, an addicted child who strayed from the family, a doctor who made a mistake or misdiagnosis. While many believe that forgiveness is a choice we make, I don't agree. My experience has taught me that forgiveness is a by-product of the healing work we do on ourselves—it's not something we "do" first that then allows us to heal. Healing doesn't begin with forgiveness; instead, it ends there.

Our current idea of forgiveness is often tied to faith and an espoused belief that healing can't begin without it. But such thinking brings undue burden to a soul already struggling, and an added pressure to "just" forgive can complicate an already challenging life experience. There's also an unspoken assumption that ties strength of faith to forgiveness. This (flawed) correlation between forgiveness and strength of faith is a fine point, but it's one worth highlighting because it doesn't have to be this way.

If forgiveness has you tied up inside, try tuning in to yourself to uncover what your own soul needs. Instead of succumbing to the pressure to forgive, honor yourself and trust your own timing. This is a more authentic way to allow your experience of forgiveness to unfold, and it's also the way you've likely experienced those other, highly personal human emotions like love and grief. You don't just say you're in love, and poof! you suddenly love someone. So why do we expect forgiveness to work this way? When we do, we set ourselves up for an inevitable fall into a defeating pattern: proclaiming forgiveness, growing frustrated, blaming, and becoming angry—only to wind up where we started, holding the hot potato of pain once more. But now, we're suffering with the added weight of feeling like we've "failed" at forgiveness.

This can be a maddening merry-go-round, and sending yourself into this painful cycle adds more work to your already full itinerary for healing. Such perceived failures may motivate you to abandon understanding altogether, which consequently may impact your ability to not only offer but receive forgiveness from others. Moreover, it may cause you to lose trust in yourself or your higher power and put at risk the opportunity to cultivate an authentic relationship with forgiveness. Authentic forgiveness is a benefit for others, but also for yourself—it's a reward that you deserve to enjoy. You know that being human is all about the *and*; life can be complicated *and* effortless, painful *and* joyful, full of grief *and* love. Because you are a human interacting with other humans, you are going to make mistakes, *and* you are going to need to forgive yourself (and mean it) time and again.

## MEETING FORGIVENESS

After an uncomfortable dialogue with an acquaintance, who told me that I "need to forgive right away in order to heal," I grew in my resolve to do no such thing. I had been given this unsolicited advice on numerous occasions, by various people in my life, all with equally varied insight into my grief. Still, whether it was from a dear friend or an acquaintance, the unified message I heard was that I needed to forgive and do so STAT, please and thank you. These were all well-meaning and kind people, and if I'm offering them a grand assumption, I would say they wanted the best for me. Yet their advice wasn't in alignment with my truth and made little sense to me until I shifted my perspective and looked at it from their perspective: they needed me to forgive because it was in alignment with their truth. Comments ranged from casually subtle to intervention-level intense, but were all born from the same place; not that I needed to forgive, but they needed me to forgive.

For a time, I didn't know what to do. I could appease them with a simple word: yes—as in, "Yes, I have forgiven." But that would have been a lie. It was the easier option, but for me, it was fake, so it wasn't the right one. Had I claimed faux-giveness, I'd probably still have those friends today, but I didn't, so I don't. Indifferent, I put the idea of forgiveness in my back pocket and went to work trying to understand the bigger beast in front of me: grief. Over these years, I gave forgiveness little thought. If someone asked or inferred, I was quick to dismiss any inquiries with a sigh: "Oh, that isn't my focus right now," I'd say, or just politely thank the inquisitor for their care. The latter, I did a lot. Then, five years after my grief first began, I finally met real forgiveness. It wasn't what I expected and didn't present as the result of a conscious decision or a resigned effort. It wasn't something I had been talking through with Amy, debating in my mind, or even noticing in my immediate awareness. It just "happened" one day while out on a hike.

## A New View

The sliced face of Yosemite's Half Dome was in front of me. Having trekked over ten miles and at over eight thousand feet above sea level, my hiking companion and I paused to hydrate and assess our next leg of the dome: the final ascent up the eastern slope. The summit stood another four hundred vertical feet above, and at a precarious forty-five-degree angle, it was understandable why the majority of people around us were opting out. Hiking to this point was victory enough, and "climbing the cables" required even more physical and mental acuity, as well as a permit issued by the National Park Service. As we approached the cables, a pair of hikers stood near the base. "I just don't trust it," one said, shaking his head. "Same," the other agreed, before turning away. For a few months each year, the National Park Service drills anchors into the smooth granite monolith. Cables are installed into the anchors and two-by-fours placed every few feet, creating a makeshift staircase and railing. I tugged on the first anchor to see if it would hold, testing it like the lap bar on a roller coaster ride. The braided cables held taut as my gloved hands grabbed on. I trusted the staircase, and I trusted myself, so, with a silent prayer, I cast my focus upward and began the final and most precarious section of the hike. "Slow and steady wins the race," I reminded myself.

Finally, after a ten-minute haul to the top, I made it. There weren't many people up there, and those who were sat quiet, eyes locked on the landscape. The majesty of it all was a lot to absorb: the sights of the valley sprawling below, the smell of the crisp, thin air, the eerie stillness of the wind, and the sounds of a few scampering marmots scavenging for bread-crumbs. My hiking partner, Chris, a man I'd started dating (with caution) a year before, was seated beside me processing his own journey up the mountain. As I reflected on my own, I saw how far I'd come, not just on that day, but every day since that ordinary Tuesday morning changed everything. There at the top of Half Dome, I felt more like myself than I ever had, and I felt proud of myself, too. I had used all the courage inside me and a whole lot of heart. I no longer doubted my own intelligence and I trusted myself completely; Chris's presence was proof that I was learning to trust others again, too.

I felt that I'd finally found my way home, but not the home of my once-before. I had stepped into my new life and was joyfully regenerating in full Technicolor wonder. I was awash in joy and overcome with gratitude for it. And in that glorious moment of silent communion, there it was. An understated but unmistakable feeling suddenly became a part of me, as if it were uploaded into my consciousness in the same way we upgrade our computer operating systems. "Me 2.0! Now with forgiveness." It wasn't a feeling of granting or accepting forgiveness, but rather an understanding of what it is and how it fits for me. I instantly understood that, for me, forgiveness wasn't necessary—it was a moot point, irrelevant to my situation. At the same time, I felt lighter and awash in a peaceful, almost foreign, sense of calm. It reminded me of my trip to the stars where I returned *knowing*, except now it was a knowing of forgiveness. In that moment and in many since, I have felt grateful to my grieving self, who didn't succumb to the pressures to faux-give. By staying in my integrity, I had found something much greater: faith in myself and an understanding of for-real, authentic forgiveness.

For those who struggle with the concept of forgiveness or feel pressure to forgive, perhaps this "moot point" perspective will help you, too. Or maybe forgiveness doesn't apply to you. Think about the people you've met in the stories I've shared. Do you believe that they need to forgive their loved ones? How do you forgive someone for a diagnosis like dementia or a brain injury? Why would you need to forgive someone for embracing who they really are? Do you need to forgive someone who is tormented by addiction or mental illness? These questions were answered for me, that day on top of Half Dome, when I understood forgiveness in a way I knew to be true for me. Maybe it isn't to you, and, of course, that's okay. I wish for you to meet forgiveness in whatever shape that takes for you, when and where and if that is your heart's desire.

## THE FOUNDATION OF FORGIVENESS

To learn how you respond to forgiveness or why someone might react as they do, cast your gaze back to your childhood. From this perspective, you'll see that your relationship with forgiveness is likely an amalgamation of many factors, starting with a foundation poured in your childhood. If you're able, answer the following questions by thinking back on your life. If your memory doesn't allow you to tap into your early years, that's okay—make note of what you recall and when it happened in your life.

1. What were you taught about forgiveness?
2. How were you taught about forgiveness?
3. Who taught you about forgiveness?
4. When was your first experience forgiving someone?
5. Why did you forgive (e.g., you were instructed, you felt obligated, you felt genuine forgiveness)?

Don't worry if you weren't able to recall much on your first try. Your subconscious may still be working to help you to answer these questions, so as you make connections and unearth memories in the days to come, be sure to add them to your notes: they may hold clues important for your healing. Even if you've not yet experienced how forgiveness feels or weren't given a formal lesson from a parent, it is likely that other sources informed your beliefs—a religious figure, teacher, friend, or even artwork or media. Perhaps a book or article influenced you; after all, the written word has been a medium of instruction longer than most.

The pressure of such social niceties isn't new; poets and parents alike have been publicly waxing prophetic on forgiving and apologizing for centuries. Among the most notable, English poet Alexander Pope in his "Essay on Criticism." First published in 1711, it has been praised and criticized for the implication that forgiveness is a marker of moral superiority. He wrote:

> Good nature and good sense must ever join;
> To err is human; to forgive divine.
> But if in noble minds some dregs remain,
> Not yet purg'd off, of spleen and sour disdain,
> Discharge that rage on more provoking crimes,
> Or fear a death in these flagitious times.

If in the eighteenth century, societies were learning that forgiveness was a divine and desirable action, it makes sense that the nineteenth century gave us instruction manuals detailing how to properly pen a flowering apology for tardiness (then known as "letters of excuse"). In modern times, we have blogs bullet-pointing steps to forgive just about anything, including how to remedy today's preschool party faux pas. Across that time, it seems that apologies and forgiveness have gone from being tools to help us care for ourselves and our relationships to a judgment of our manners, and thereby our societal status. It's no wonder many of today's parents intervene quickly and guide their preschoolers with prompting: "Say I'm sorry"; "Say it's okay." Though well-intended, such prompting acts as a disservice, creating a child who "parrots," not one who understands. Prompting and parroting may help secure another playdate, but it doesn't provide the parties involved an opportunity for autonomy over their feelings. Even as research regarding authentic apologizing makes its way to mainstream outlets, it doesn't seem to have made its way to the sandbox just yet.

But regardless of where, how, and what you learned, the belief system formed around forgiveness impacts your worldview, shaping your understanding of not only how you are expected to behave, but how the world should behave toward you. For example, you may have been taught that you need to seek forgiveness if you inflict harm upon someone. A common way to seek forgiveness is to ask for it by apologizing to the person you've hurt. For some, this is a direct ask: "I'm sorry; will you please forgive me?" For others, it's indirect, and often comes with an assumption that "I'm sorry" is a complete apology the recipient is obligated to accept (spoiler: it isn't). If you have a healthy relationship with forgiveness and feel confident giving and receiving appropriate apologies— awesome! But if not, understanding how you learned to offer and accept apologies (or not) may help to explain aspects of your relationship with forgiveness today.

### The Absent Apology

Perhaps you aren't interested in how to give or receive an authentic apology, but how to *get* one. Unlike those grieving a physical death, it is still possible for you to be offered an apology because your loved one is still alive. You may feel you deserve an apology, are entitled to an apology, or require one in order to move forward. If you were offered an unsuitable apology, you may be waiting on a better one, or perhaps you feel as though it's the least your loved one could do for you after all the pain they have caused. But fixating on an inauthentic or absent apology is a ticket back to external hope and a focus on things that are not within your power. Though you may long for an apology worthy of your pain, it isn't the missing piece you may believe it to be. Even if you want the apology because you plan to accept it, forgive them, and move on, it's not something you actually need in order to do so. Yes, an authentic apology may be what you want, but it isn't what you *need* in order to forgive, and it isn't a prerequisite to your healing. Remember that you are in charge of your healing and are generating a new life for yourself. If an absent apology is a barrier preventing you from moving forward with joy, spend some time on the next exercise and generate the apology you deserve.

---

### Exercise 19 | All Apologies

Connect again to your heart and write yourself the heart-felt letter of apology you long for. Write the apology from the perspective of your loved one, opening with Dear (Your Name) and concluding by signing their name. Let it flow out of you and onto the paper as naturally as possible. Use your grievances as a guide and write an apology for each one. When you're finished, consider sharing your letter with a therapist or trusted friend who can not only serve as a witness to your experience, but help you to process it as well.

---

As demonstrated by the snake in Aesop's forgiveness fable, it's not only your choice how you accept an apology, but it's your choice if you do so at all. While it may feel counterintuitive, Aesop's fable illustrates that whether you accept or decline an apology doesn't imply you are forgetting or forgiving. In better understanding apologies, we can now shift our perspective once more and review them in relation to forgiveness.

## F.

A year after Half Dome, with my newly upgraded operating system on board, I felt confident in my relationship with forgiveness—until a nagging question surfaced in my mind. Much like the original question that had prompted me to this path in the first place ("Why was my grief different?"), a new one was nudging me in the same way. This time the question was, "How can we find forgiveness?" Though I tried to tuck that question in my newly vacated back pocket, it wouldn't stay there. Instead, it roamed the reaches of my mind as fragmented thoughts throughout the day and as abstract dreams at night, just as hope had a few years before. After working so hard to get to life on the other side, dissecting forgiveness wasn't on my to-do list. I didn't think it needed to be done!

Even though this line of thinking had Amy's name all over it, I knew she wasn't to blame. Early on, she had supported my position about faux-giveness and suggested that it may even create more mounds of frustration, but we hadn't since returned to the topic. It was the still, small voice inside that was calling me into action, and I knew why. I had hacked my way to forgiveness, and now my higher self was calling me out for the shortcut. The new acquisition of forgiveness had been more than just highly effective for me—it was a true gift, since it wasn't something I had aspired to. But along the way to it, I had come to know so many ambiguous grievers who *were* earnestly trying to find forgiveness or, worse, may never fully find it because they were living with faux-giveness. This thought initiated a feeling of deep obligation, not only to my higher self, but to my brethren of ambiguous grievers whose stories had helped me in countless ways. Still, this scab wasn't one I was willing to pick, and besides, I didn't have time. As an ambiguous grief guide, my days were full, and a diversion down the path to forgiveness wasn't part of my itinerary. No sooner had I made that decision, when my editor suggested, "Some connective tissue is missing, since forgiveness isn't the same experience for everyone. There's more to explore here." I knew she was right, and even though I didn't want this assignment, maybe I needed it. I dried my tears, cleared my calendar, and began to examine my relationship with the other F word from different angles.

## Digging Deep

Since our meeting at Sex Monster Camp, Maya had become a dear and trusted friend whose support and advice I'd come to value. I recalled how she had articulated forgiveness when I was ruminating on it during one of our early chats. She suggested that maybe it wasn't even applicable in the first place. This confused me, coming from her, because she herself had been so egregiously wronged. She reframed her comment for me, suggesting not that I think about "the how" of forgiveness, but rather to think about "the what"—what was it, *exactly*, that people needed to forgive and, what, exactly, holds them back. I didn't know it at the time, but this invitation from Maya was a guiding light on my path, one that she had already discovered along hers. But though she offered me this flame from her wisdom, I wasn't ready until years later, when it flickered to life and became a lantern for me, too. This reminds me of the Zen proverb: "When the student is ready, the teacher appears."

Even though I wasn't able to receive Maya's insight when she first offered it, I returned to the sentiment she'd offered and I'd waved off, now curious if it held more clues. As it turned out, it did. The "what" I had thought I needed for forgiving was made up of many (many!) grievances that piled on top of one another many (many!) layers deep. Not unlike a mountain or other great rock formation, blasting through each layer takes fortitude and a certain resolve to uncover what's lurking beneath. Regardless of where you are in relation to forgiveness, it may be helpful, or at the very least cathartic, for you to work through the first few layers by answering formally and filing your grievances on what harm *exactly* you need to forgive.

Again, by writing this out, you aren't just creating a mental list—you are connecting your heart to hand, which creates space for your feelings to flow out of you and onto the paper. **Big disclaimer:** This exercise has the potential to release a torrent of memories and create and recall emotions, so proceed with care. The best conditions under which to attempt this exercise are when you:

- are alone and free from interruption
- are in a safe, quiet, comfortable physical space
- are in a grounded and stable emotional space
- have time afterward to implement your favorite self-care practices
- have someone available for a call or session to help you process what you've unearthed (for extra reinforcement, consider asking your mental wellness professional if they are open to the idea of guiding you through it)

## *Exercise 20 | Mount Grievance*

Think about your loved one and the activating event that sent you on your journey of ambiguous grief. As you do, acknowledge any "hard" feelings that you sense, such as hurt, hate, pain, blame, anguish, embarrassment, anxiety, regret, or shame. The purpose of this exercise isn't to drain your emotional energy. Instead, once you eventually mine your way to the bottom, you may find intent buried underneath it all. Once you dismantle your own mountain and take time to inspect the foundation, your grievances may feel a little different.

**Step 1:** List your grievances and the emotions you associate with them in your notebook. Remember, identifying and naming your emotions is crucial.

**Step 2:** Excavating the thoughts behind those emotions is the next step, so return to your list. Identify the thoughts behind each emotion, writing as freely as you are able. Tip: the word "because" may be a good prompt to draw out the "whats" and "whys."

Two helpful examples:

Humiliation—I am filing a grievance because I felt humiliated. My thoughts behind this feeling say, "The person who had taken an oath to love and care for me willingly chose to engage in behaviors that were directly opposed to that oath, and others knew about it, but I didn't." "Other women acted as accomplices and knew of my existence, so they must think they have something I don't."

"I am so naïve; I didn't have a clue." "I was too
trusting; it was happening under my nose." "I bet
they talked about me when they were together."

**Scorn**—I am filing a grievance because I feel
scornful. My thoughts behind this feeling say,
"My child chose to cut me from her life without
talking to me about it, and I am scornful toward
her and myself." "Other relatives must have told
her lies and untruths about me." "She has made a
mockery of me." "Maybe I am the horrible father
she thinks I am."

When you've finished filing your grievances, shift your perspective once again. This time, you'll have help from a tool
used by the modern-day criminal justice system. When
determining wrongdoing and a proportionate consequence,
the law looks for *intent*. Defined as "the resolve or determination with which a person willfully acts to commit a transgression," intent is categorized into three types:

- General—an action performed (e.g., the boy
  stepped on the snake while playing)
- Specific—an action performed that has a motive
  and requires preplanning and predisposition (e.g.,
  the man took an axe to harm the snake and did)
- Constructive—an action of general intent performed that consequently causes harm, and even
  though one could have reasonably expected the
  outcome, they legitimately didn't intend for it to
  happen (e.g., the snake bit the boy and it killed him)

**Step 3:** For the final step of this exercise, review your list of grievances through the lens of intent. Does your list of grievances indicate intent to harm you, emotionally or otherwise? Determine if the intent was general, specific, or constructive.

Depending on your experience with this exercise, your findings may cause you to change course. Perhaps a different path materializes, a new perspective requires rerouting, or you more clearly see the barriers in your way. For some, the distance to forgiveness is direct; for example, if your loved one didn't have a choice in their activating event, and you know that there was no intent to harm you, an apology and forgiveness may not be necessary. Not only that, but if the loss of your loved one is due to mental illness or a medical condition like Alzheimer's, you can't expect them to ask for forgiveness because they may not be able to.

Conversely, if your loved one *did* have intent, the path to forgiveness is likely less clear. For instance, for those who had their trust broken by their loved one, this exercise may have helped to reveal that you don't know what grievances to file because you don't know what you don't know. Sometimes, the only thing worse than knowing that your loved one acted with specific intent and disregard for your feelings is knowing that you don't know the half of it. Regardless of which intent best applies to your situation, this exercise may help to unearth any false narratives that you've created, about yourself or others, as found in the above examples "I'm so naïve" and "she has made a mockery of me." Imagine yourself sweeping away those false narratives and cleaning up your emotional excavation site. As you do, you may find clarity in what remains, the actions and the intent of your loved one, and potentially, a different perspective on forgiveness.

---

## LOVE AND FEAR

Before you go on, take a moment to reflect on the last exercise and tune in to how you are feeling. Overall, are your feelings more aligned with love or fear? Here's how each of these might feel:

- Love—warm, peaceful, relieving, safe, joyful
- Fear—hurt, angry, sad, unsafe, afraid

When I looked at my own list, I found that my mountain of grievances was layered in false narratives, and fear:

- Fear of what others have thought or are thinking of me
- Fear of what could have happened
- Fear of not knowing what else I didn't know
- Fear of losing love
- Fear of an unknown future
- Fear of never understanding why
- Fear of forgiveness

Not only was I surprised to discover so much fear, but further reflection revealed that I had been fearful of forgiveness early on because I simply hadn't known how to handle it. While I didn't give into pressure to *faux*-give, I put it in my back pocket because I didn't have the tools to work through it. After looking more closely, I was better able to understand its nuances and articulate some valuable insights that I hadn't yet connected. While I doubted the necessity of doubling back and searching for something that I already had on board, I'm grateful that I did because I picked up new insights. Among them, a rock-hard reminder that forgiving isn't synonymous with *forgetting*, nor does it disqualify your grief or signal to others that you're "okay" with how you were harmed. Also, perhaps the most disheartening understanding was that in our pressure-to-forgive culture, many travelers also experience feelings of guilt when they don't "find forgiveness"—which brings me to the final perspective on forgiveness for your consideration. Though it may feel counterintuitive to your pursuit, I encourage you to be willing to examine it as an option, even if it may be frightening. But, like anything that scares you—monsters under your childhood bed, or a midlife career change—you can minimize its power by being daring enough to take a look and uncover what's hiding there.

## Rethink and Resign

Though a search for missing "connective tissue" was the only reason I looked under the bed, I'm glad I did. In doing this, many paths to forgiveness began to take shape, all beneficial to my own learning and, hopefully, yours too.

Whether derived from an internal desire or external pressure, finding forgiveness may feel like one more "thing" you need to do. If so, it's no wonder, since "finding forgiveness" has been part of our vernacular over several centuries in books, magazines, lectures, religious studies, and beyond. However, just as rethinking recovery helped me to discover regeneration as a more appropriate lens, try to rethink forgiveness in the same way.

**Instead of trying to find forgiveness, allow forgiveness to find you.** Calling off the search doesn't mean you aren't a good person or that you're somehow morally less-than. It doesn't mean you are apathetic, giving up, or coldhearted either. It means that you are shifting from a state of forcing to a state of allowing because, much like love itself, forgiveness can't be hurried or willed into being. Like the experience of love and all things found in nature, forgiveness also unfolds naturally, on its own divine timeline, not yours. So, if you're open to *forgiveness finding you*, you need to do nothing more than declare that you are open to it, then take action by giving yourself the very best care possible in the meantime.

In resigning your quest to find forgiveness, you create time and space to focus on yourself and what grows your joy. You can use this newfound energy to feed your intellect, cultivate your curiosities, and nourish the parts of you that are still healing. These are the provisions that you need as you live life on the other side of loss, with or without forgiveness. Though the feeling of forgiveness is described in many different ways,

it's one that's unmistakable. If you aren't sure if you have forgiven, or think maybe you have but don't know for certain,
then you haven't—you don't know it until you experience
it, and then you know! Whether you find it, or it finds you,
or neither, remember: not everyone meets forgiveness, and
that's okay, too.

---

## Forgive and Remember

It's possible that you may conclude forgiveness is irrelevant
to your healing or that exploring it further will cost you
more emotional effort than you want to spend. Perhaps
you find that it isn't required (because it's not applicable in
the first place), or that forgiveness is necessary and needed
for your healing. The latter may be especially relevant for
those who seek to reconcile their relationship, especially
if trust has been broken. In such cases, a mutual understanding of forgiveness may serve as a helpful tool for
rebuilding. Moreover, what you find out about your own
feelings of forgiveness may evolve over time, which was
the case for Diane, whom you met in Chapter 3. Separated
after infidelity and deciding on divorce, she summoned
the courage to face her fear of the unknown. As she examined her foundation and spent years working on herself,
she was able to quietly observe that her husband was doing
the same, and she made an important discovery: though it
was deeply buried, she eventually uncovered a firm foundation of love. Five years later, upon it, she built a new life
with her old/new husband.

"Initially, forgiveness seemed impossible," she said. "He had betrayed my trust and our relationship. More than that, he broke our covenant, something I thought we treasured equally. After my anger abated, I recognized how hard he was working to face the consequences of his actions—individual therapy to understand the root, group therapy for accountability, and weeks-long therapy intensives coalescing the two.

"I was certain that no 'reason' could explain his choices or lessen the trauma he'd inflicted, but in doing my own emotional work and continuing in couples' therapy, I began to see his actions from a different standpoint. He had acted out in ways that had hurt me tremendously, but it wasn't because of anything I had done or didn't do; it was about what had happened to him. He'd spent a lifetime denying the pain and suffering he'd endured in childhood, and his actions as an adult, as my husband, were a result of that. Understanding this changed my perspective, and I became open to forgiving him. That didn't mean we were going to move back in together or even be friends, but I was willing, and that alone was a big shift. I didn't know what a future relationship may look like for us—if anything—but I knew that the relationship, as it had been, was gone."

Inspired by that realization, Diane and her husband held a ceremony. Much like my own faux-u-neral, it proved transformative not only to her but to their relationship as well. "It was heartbreaking," she said. "Burying our wedding rings symbolized that our marriage had died. The rings were reminders of broken vows that destroyed my trust. Even after a couple of years working toward recovery, this was such an emotionally difficult day, but it was an important marker for us both.

"A year later, we held another ceremony for ourselves with new rings. This was an important reframing for me, especially, to honor the commitment to the new relationship we were building. It wasn't just a continuation; it was an honoring of something new and hopeful. We exchanged our vows as two very different people than the first time we said 'I do.'"

Diane shared what she ultimately learned about forgiveness: "In recovery, my experience of forgiveness had shifted yet again; forgiveness is not what I thought it was. It's not when you let someone off the hook. It's when you wish them well in spite of how they've hurt you, and it's when you can see them as more than their betrayal. Though better understanding trauma helped me to forgive, I can't imagine I will ever forget. Nor do I want to. On occasion, we'll visit the burial site of our old marriage, and it's always sad, but the truth is, it's a part of us, too."

---

## FRIENDING FORGIVENESS

Whether or not intent helps you to discover love or fear buried in your foundation, the exercise is meant as a tool to help you gain clarity on forgiveness and what, if anything, it means for you. If nothing else, perhaps this unannounced pit stop assuaged any lingering feelings you hadn't yet addressed or has given you pause for thought. Whether you have befriended the other F word or strengthened your resolve against its necessity, I hope that, despite whatever societal pressures you have, you feel more informed and confident in your position.

For me, this diversion helped me to find facets of forgiveness that I would have otherwise missed or hadn't quite articulated. Namely:

- Saying "I'm sorry" isn't an incantation used to summon forgiveness, any more than saying "I love you" bestows love (yet we expect this of one another often).
- Not succumbing to societal pressures to say you forgive doesn't mean that you are holding a grudge or making a power grab. Rather, you are being honest, speaking your truth, and standing in your integrity (and that's more important than anything found in articles on etiquette!).
- All aspects of forgiveness are your prerogative: if, when, and how you forgive, and even what you deem an appropriate amends (the offender doesn't set the terms for rectifying the harm to your relationship—you do).
- You can reframe your relationship with forgiveness whenever you choose.
- Forgiveness is not something to fear, but to befriend.
- Forgiveness isn't something we have to find; it is an experience that may find us.

### Finders Keepers

Whatever you decide to do with forgiveness is up to you: search for it or not, keep it or share it. For example, if you forgive, the choice is also yours if you share that or not. You don't *need* to inform someone of your forgiveness to make it true; deciding to keep it private won't invalidate its presence. For some, not declaring their forgiveness is not only the best choice, but the only choice. If you feel that reconnecting with your loved one may cause you more pain, pull you back into the cycle of hope, or jeopardize your progress, consider creating a private ceremony of forgiveness with a trusted witness instead. Whether you are the forgiver or the forgiven, you have autonomy over your choice to pursue, give, receive, decline, forgive, or not forgive—in any combination. Whether you kick it over, pick it up, or leave it be, only you know if forgiveness is a tool you need in your healing—or not. It may also be one you choose not to pursue or decide to investigate at a later time, and, in that case, you can get started by returning to any of the vantage points we've explored together. Yes, it's scary, but trust yourself to find your way through—I know you can do it. After all, you've made it this far! An important note: Forgiveness is an intimate act, so the details—if, when, and how you do it or not—is nobody's business but yours. Perhaps if we stop regarding apologies and forgiveness as casual assumptions, we'd gain the clarity to see their innate personal nature. If you wouldn't ask someone how they explore their sexuality, don't ask them for details about their forgiveness. How's *that* for etiquette?

## LIFE ON THE OTHER SIDE

As we move toward our departure point, you may experience a bittersweet feeling. While the path to healing has been a long and winding, "are we there yet?" kind of trip, it's also been one that has allowed you many opportunities to explore who you are, what you believe, and how you want to move forward. It's taken a lot of energy to dig through the many emotional layers that brought you here in the first place and to get you to this point. Whether you thought it would be better or worse than it turned out, it probably wasn't quite what you expected. Perhaps what you thought you needed or wanted wasn't necessary to your healing after all, such as forgiveness, apologies, or the reconciliation of your relationship (or not). But none of that alone is what controls your healing—what does is whether you acknowledged your truth, your grief, your pain, and your desire to take action toward healing. It also matters that you didn't cut corners or rely on others to do the work for you, but that you put in the time and energy to heal your soulbroken self. Just as important is how you finish what you've started—how gracefully you move into life on the other side of your loss and how you respond to unexpected truths and your new reality.

As you prepare for this journey to end, remember that a new one awaits just ahead. Life on the other side of loss is yours for the making. In all you've endured, I hope you have found, as I did, that no matter what awaits you on your path ahead, you have the tools you need. If you're not afraid to use them, you'll be okay! That's because you have already traversed a dark and lonely trail and took care of yourself along the way. You need not fear any path or worry about any surprise or truth discovered because you can trust yourself, not someone outside of yourself, to get you through it.

One such truth relates to your grief: as you move forward, your grief is going with you. While some of you have known this, it may come as a surprise to others. But it isn't anything for you to fear. Your grief from this loss is a part of you now, and, just like your own body, grief changes with time, shifting in shape and weight. Some days you will feel its size more than others, and on occasion you may even think it's gone entirely. But it's not—it's just not on the surface as it once was. How you take care of your grief determines how you carry it; it can be a blemish you abhor or a beauty mark you embrace. Your grief is a part of you now, and, like any other part of you, it's your responsibility to manage it.

It's understandable if you perceived that getting to life on the other side of loss meant that you would be free of your grief. Along your path, you may have thought that if you could just let go of love, then you could get to acceptance and find healing. After finding meaning, you may have assumed that you'd now exchange grief for healing and begin life in recovery. But that didn't happen, and you still carried love. By digging to emotional bedrock, you discovered your feelings on forgiveness and may have conquered your fears—only to learn that grief was still hanging on, though so, too, was love. Though they may seem an unlikely duo, love and grief are loyal companions, to each other and to you. So, as you begin to joyfully live life on the other side of your loss, accept that grief will be there, too—and you'll be okay.

Over the years, you'll manage it as you might any other part of you that needs attention, and may find that it isn't as debilitating as it once was. You'll learn to tend to your grief just as tenderly as you did your love, and in that find that your love is still with you, too. Though it's not what it once was, like grief, it doesn't slip into past tense and go away, not fully anyhow. Grief isn't part of you because you "loved" someone, but because you "love" someone who is no longer with you as they once were. Love isn't something that ceases to exist because it's no longer in its former form, and though that love may no longer be active and growing, it doesn't mean that it isn't still there and doesn't deserve to be acknowledged.

As your path unfolds, even years later, there may be days when the loss of your loved one overwhelms you and grief throws you off balance. But every time you tend to it instead of ignoring it, you are growing closer to your grief instead of ghosting it. As you get better acquainted with grief, with or without forgiveness, you understand that every time you honor this part of you, your soul heals a little bit more. You learn, too, that you cannot be angry at grief for being grief any more than you can be angry at love for being love. They are yin and yang, equal opposites, and are with you because, in the end, grief is love's invoice.

# Unpacking

"Remember, we are all but travelers here."

—MARY MACKILLOP

It's nearly time for us to part ways, and though the top of a mountain may seem an unlikely place for us to end our journey, it's as far as I can take you. Think of the next part of your journey as a "self-guided" excursion, where you'll write your own itinerary and explore the personal points of interest best suited to you. You may head in the direction of friends and family, seeking to recharge by connecting with loved ones, or maybe you've kicked over enough rocks for the time being and need to retreat to your safe space and decompress. Maybe you feel inspired to revisit a hobby you once enjoyed or entertain the thought of something entirely new. Whatever it may be, your upcoming solo expedition offers an infinite number of itineraries! This is a thrilling notion for some and terrifying for others. If there is no obvious next step for you, or you don't know how to decide, this point of your journey may feel overwhelming. I understand, because I felt that way, too. What I found was that looking back can help to inform where you go next, so the final exercise on your guided itinerary is intended to help you do just that. As seasoned travelers know, no trip truly ends until you've unpacked, so let's huddle up one final time and do that together. You've come a long way since we first set out, so as you assess your notes and unpack the journey, do so with a specific intention: looking at where you've been and what you've learned for clues on where you might want to guide yourself next.

---

*Exercise 21 | Unpacking*

When you're ready to make sense of what you've learned, return to the beginning of the book. Flip through each chapter and jot down your biggest insights from each stop, the "takeaways" that resonated most. Even if they feel inconsequential, I assure you they are not. Think of each learning as a glowing lantern along your personal path. In identifying your growth from each stop, you're lighting each lantern. At ground level, they serve as individual trail markers, helping to light your way from one stop to the next. But when viewed from a higher elevation, their collective form projects the illuminated path you've created. Seeing your path in this way can help bring focus to where you've been and inform your way forward. Be sure to inspect your journal for clues, paying special attention to your notes on tools and exercises. In addition, make note of any patterns you detect—for example, any underlying themes or recurring feelings. Then, while it's still fresh in your mind, log your final journal entry by summarizing your journey, starting with your activating event and noting your lanterns at each stop. Though your path is unique, it may one day be valuable to others called to this quest—so grab a pencil and get comfortable!

## THE LIGHT INSIDE YOU

Wherever you go next, you now have the benefit of viewing your own path in its full form. The parade of lanterns signaling your route have gifted you with souvenirs of wisdom, too. For me, my final insight is one I reflect upon daily. You recall my first was discovering that what makes the experience of ambiguous grief different is that the person being grieved is still alive, but the relationship has drastically *changed* from what it once was. My last insight was far more unexpected, and only perceptible when viewed in aggregate; it was that *ambiguous grief changed me drastically, too.*

Ultimately, the experience transformed every part of me, mind, body, and soul. It introduced me to incredible souls I wouldn't have otherwise known and connected me back to my own. But it wasn't until I found my way through and was eventually able to look at my illuminated path from the mountaintop vantage point that I recognized this truth. Even more, I found this wasn't unique to me because, on some level, all travelers navigating ambiguous grief are changed by it. How it changes you depends on your own path and the insight you've gained along the way, but like love, grief, and forgiveness, the "how" is personal and unique to you.

As you reflect, give yourself time to process your experience, and, as always, talk it through with your Amy or another trusted member of your care team. The answers may not be immediately obvious, so grant yourself grace and trust that a part of you *already* knows the way. Even if it has yet to be revealed, believe that it will be, because the biggest lantern of all is housed inside of you. Though your loss may have caused you to unplug from life and your inner light may have dimmed, it was never meant to stay that way, and with each and every noble stride toward healing, you have already reconnected yourself in many ways.

Perhaps you have connected to your grief, yourself, your higher power, and to others. Little by little, your soulbroken self may also tether itself to something even greater—a higher level of consciousness or the very source of love itself. As you reestablish these connections, you rekindle the light within until, *zap!* you're firmly moored. In continuing to turn down the volume on external noise, and as long as you are doing your part and listening, you can amplify your own inner knowing and trust that the light within will always guide you forward. As you do, and as other travelers do the same, perhaps we will collectively improve our relationship with grief. Maybe then it will be perceived less as a mangy, militant houseguest we fear, and more as a venerable mentor we appreciate, one whom we can expect to visit once in a while and one who helps us to grow into our highest self. But in order to help bring about a world where grief is recognized as a worthy stamp in your earthly passport, you'll need to make one more decision—whether to share your journey. Grief is a difficult terrain to traverse, and it isn't always easy for others to hear, especially when saddled with shame, embarrassment, or confusion. Just remember that doesn't disqualify you from your right to share your journey, if you decide to do so.

I suspect that this has plagued explorers for all time—from native stargazers and nascent seafarers to modern-day astronauts and aquanauts. As with them, whether or not you choose to share your discoveries—where you've been and what you've learned—is solely up to you. Sharing something so personal is a vulnerable act that may not be easy; it certainly wasn't for me. You may feel afraid, not knowing how you'll be received, or you may even face admonishment (or worse) within your community for doing so. But just as you have autonomy over your love and forgiveness, you also have agency over your own journey through grief, so it's your choice if you share what you've learned along the way.

Like the travelers you met throughout the book, your experience has transformed you, too. Whatever your path forward, it's my hope that you will embrace your grief with gratitude and continue forward in full Technicolor. The path I charted and guided you through is but one among many, and my *deep* hope is that it has served you during a difficult time. My even *deeper* hope is that by sharing my path, you have discovered a lantern or two of your own and feel less alone than you did before our time together. If that is true for you, my *deepest* hope is that you are regenerating and will someday share a flame from your lantern to help another. In doing so, perhaps together we can help to light the way for the procession of soulbroken sojourners en route, showing by example that ambiguous grief isn't something to cover up or overcome, but rather something that was born from love, transformed by loss, and now resides deep within, a passageway to a precious and sacred part of us.

And why wouldn't we want it to be?

# Fifteen Re-routing Tools

Navigating the gnarled nuances of ambiguous grief is a challenging experience, so having the right tools throughout the process is an important component of your healing. The following are fifteen of my favorites, all of which we explored throughout this book and can be used at various points along your path. However, this is not an exhaustive list, so be mindful of what other tools you find helpful and be sure to add them to this list.

**Declaraction**—Getting clear on your desires and declaring what you want is an important function in life, regardless of whether you are grieving. Declaration followed by action to support your words is needed to move you out of an emotional or physical state you don't want to stay in. Declare and then *act* (and repeat).

**Faux-u-neral**—Without a standard model to ritualize and recognize the death of your relationship, you may feel unvalidated in your grief. Reconcile your reality with a ceremony or ritual that is meaningful to you. Doing so can help you honor your ending by providing an opportunity for your grief to be witnessed by others and be an expression of the love you have for the relationship that has changed or died.

**Forgiveness**—Societal, religious, and familial influences will likely dictate your relationship with "the other F word." Whether you are on a quest to find forgiveness or are content to allow forgiveness to find you, exploring your relationship with apologies and forgiveness may offer keen insight in your healing (or not).

**Goggles**—As you grow in your internal hope, practice envisioning your life ahead. Dedicate a quiet few minutes each day to closing your eyes and envisioning your desired future. Be sure that you are the  focus of the experience, and don't get too bogged down in the details (on a beach laughing in the sun is detail enough). Once you have the vision in your mind's eye, tap into how it feels and allow that feeling to wash over you, working up to a minute, if possible.

**Intention**—Mentally determining how you want to proceed can help you to chart your course and guide your behavior.

Intentions rooted in self-love and self-care are important; for example, your intention for healing may be to treat yourself gently or interact with your loved one with kindness. Use the tool of intention to guide you  through your overall journey, during specific stages, and in daily interactions. Recall your intention early and often to guide you along the way.

**Intuition**—The deep part of yourself that guides you throughout life, acting like your own internal GPS, intuition will warn or affirm you and is often felt in the gut. The  more you check in with yourself and follow your intuition's signals, the more you'll grow in trust with this part of yourself. Practice tuning in to your intuition by getting quiet with daily "gut checks," and learn to find other ways your intuition signals you to pay attention.

**Love**—Practice showing yourself love in the form of self-care and compassion, and as you do, you will better show love toward others. When you aren't sure what tool to use, reach for love. Your intention can be love, you can find meaning in love, you can build your Recovery Roster with love, and so on. Speak from love and act in love, for others and for yourself. Easier said than done—but it's a decision that leaves little regret.

**Meaning**—When used at the right time, this tool can help ease your suffering and bring insights into focus. Meaning may also provide a sense of relief, but if it's rushed or prescribed too soon, it won't last. In order for meaning to "stick," acceptance must be securely anchored.

**Meditation**—Practice being present by quieting your mind and allowing focus on your breath. This age-old practice calms and collects your nervous system, reducing anxiety and stress, among many other benefits. Dedicate a few minutes a day and work up to more. Remember, it's not about not thinking: it's training your mind to quiet the blabbering child within.

**My People**—Individuals who understand your loss and are working through their grief as well. More important than parallel grief timelines is your shared activating event. As the nuances of loss vary depending on the nature of the loss, finding others who can relate is key. Your People are especially valuable early on, acting like a "Special Ops" team; you can help one another with the difficult onset and most trying times. Note that it's okay if Your People are not on your Recovery Roster, especially if you're not

compatible energetically and they are no longer additive to your healing.

**Recovery Roster**—As you move into a space of healing where your days are no longer dominated by your grief, it's important to be intentional about your relationships. As you are stepping into your life "post-loss," continued self-care is paramount. Part of  that includes an honest assessment of with whom you spend your time. Protect your energy during this delicate period by being discerning; how you feel after spending time with them is a good clue.

**Sort and File**—When you experience increased frustration, identify the source of your angst and examine whether it is something that is within your power. This will allow you to gain clarity on areas of focus that pre-serve your energy instead of draining it.  This is an especially helpful tool when you find yourself cycling in and out of hope, or when you feel disappointed or anxious over your loved one's words or actions.

**Soul Salve**—Pay attention to what is heal-ing for you during the many stages of your grief. Art, birding, books, exercise, garden-ing, knitting, learning, meditation, music, reading, religious studies, outdoor activities, podcasts, puzzles, scrapbooking, traveling, and writing are just a few soul salve remedies.

**Time**—It is common for grievers to mark time as happening either "before" or "after" their loss. While it is true that healing takes time, the passing of time is not a viable single strategy for healing. As time moves forward from your activating event, pair other supportive tools with it to engage with your grief in a healthy way.

**Write**—Expressing your experience in written form helps to move your thoughts and emotions out of your mind and onto your tablet or paper. In connecting your head to your heart through your hand, writing allows for a safe space to release and reflect.

# INTRODUCTION

**Ambiguous Loss**
Ambiguous Loss website
Department of Family Social Science
University of Minnesota
www.ambiguousloss.com

# CHAPTER 1

**Mental Wellness**
Find a Therapist: www.findatherapist.com
*Psychology Today*: www.psychologytoday.com

# CHAPTER 2

**The Omega Institute**
Rhinebeck, NY
845.266.4444
www.eomega.org

**TED Talks**
www.TED.com

**Mindfulness and Meditation**
Mindful Communications: www.mindful.org
Headspace app: www.headspace.com
Calm app: www.calm.com

Resources

**Alzheimer's Association**
800.272.3900
www.alz.org

**Caregiver Action Network**
202.454.3970
www.caregiveraction.org

## CHAPTER 3

**The Meadows**
Wickenburg, AZ
866.331.3368 (U.S.)
928.668.1999 (outside U.S.)
Themeadows.com

**The Center for Prolonged Grief**
Columbia University School of Social Work
212.851.2107
www.prolongedgrief.columbia.edu

## CHAPTER 4

**Tameka Means**
Tamekacmeans@gmail.com
www.prisonlovemindset.com

## CHAPTER 5

**Rythmia Life Advancement Center**
Guanacaste, Costa Rica
844.236.5674
www.rythmia.com

**Johns Hopkins Psychedelic Research**
www.hopkinspsychedelic.org

**Multidisciplinary Association for Psychedelic Studies**
www.maps.org

**Nar-Anon Family Groups**
800.477.6291
www.nar-anon.org

**Al-Anon Family Groups**
888.4AL.ANON (888.425.2666)
www.al-anon.org

## CHAPTER 6
www.transfamilies.org
www.pflag.org

## CHAPTER 7

**National Park Service**
www.nps.gov

# NOTES

## INTRODUCTION: THEN

1. Elisabeth Kübler-Ross. *On Death and Dying.* New York: The McMillan Company, 1969.
2. Pauline Boss. *Ambiguous Loss: Learning to Live with Unresolved Grief.* Cambridge, MA: Harvard University Press, 1999.

## CHAPTER 1: ACTIVATING EVENTS, ESTRANGEMENT, AND INTENTION

1. Caudle and Sarazin, Ambiguous Grief Process Model. 2018.
2. Sigmund Freud. *Mourning and Melancholy.* 1917.

## CHAPTER 2: THE FEELING STATE OF GRIEF, COGNITIVE DECLINE, AND MINDING YOUR MIND

1. James W. Pennebaker. "Writing about Emotional Experiences as a Therapeutic Process." *Psychological Science* 8, no. 3 (1997): 162–66. http://www.jstor.org/stable/40063169
2. Aristotle. *Rhetoric*, Book II, 12.2.
3. Paul Ekman, Wallace V. Friesen, and Phoebe C. Ellsworth. *Emotion in the Human Face: Guidelines for Research and an Integration of Findings.* New York: Pergamon Press, 1972.
4. Robert Plutchik. "Emotions: A General Psychoevolutionary Theory." In *Approaches to Emotion*, edited by Klaus Scherer and Paul Ekman, 197–219. Hillsdale, NJ: Erlbaum; 1984.
5. Lisa Feldman Barrett. *How Emotions Are Made.* New York: Houghton Mifflin Harcourt, 2017.

# Notes

6. Brené Brown. *Daring Greatly: How the Courage to Be Vulnerable Transforms the Way We Live, Love, Parent, and Lead.* New York: Penguin Random House, 2012.
7. Thich Nhat Hanh's Tea Meditation | *Super Soul Sunday* | Oprah Winfrey Network. http://www.youtube.com/user/OWN
8. Jon Kabat-Zinn. *Wherever You Go, There You Are: Mindfulness Meditation in Everyday Life.* New York: Hachette, 1994.
9. Britta K. Hölzel et al. "Mindfulness Practice Leads to Increases in Regional Brain Gray Matter Density." *Psychiatry Research: Neuroimaging* 191, no. 1 (2011): 36–43. doi:10.1016/j.pscychresns.2010.08.006
10. Britta K. Hölzel et al. "Mindfulness Practice Leads to Increases in Regional Brain Gray Matter Density." *Psychiatry Research: Neuroimaging* 191, no. 1 (2011): 36–43. doi:10.1016/j.pscychresns.2010.08.006
11. Brigid Shulte. "Harvard Neuroscientist: Meditation Not Only Reduces Stress, Here's How It Changes Your Brain." *Washington Post,* May 26, 2015.

## CHAPTER 3: HOPE, PERSONAL POWER, AND THE WOMEN OF SEX MONSTER CAMP

1. Epictetus. *Enchiridion.*
2. Benjamin Gardner, Phillippa Lally, and Jane Wardle. "Making Health Habitual: The Psychology of 'Habit-Formation' and General Practice." *British Journal of General Practice* 62, no. 605 (2012): 664–666. doi:10.3399/bjgp12X659466

## CHAPTER 4: INTERNAL HOPE, IMPRISONMENT, AND WHAT ELSA FORGOT

1. M. K. Gandhi. "My Inconsistency." *Young India Newsletter,* November 17, 1921, p. 661.
2. www.fatherly.com/news/new-study-reveals-most-popular-disney -song-ever-but-whats-up-with-the-rest-of-the-list/
3. https://trainingmag.com/rules-of-engagement-guidelines-for -effective-team-interaction/

## CHAPTER 5: THE BRIDGE TO RECOVERY, ADDICTION, RECONCILIATION, AND RITUALS

1. Proceedings of the National Academy of Sciences of the United States (PNAS) Vol. 116 (23), 11207–11212. https://doi.org/10.1073/pnas.1902174116, May 7, 2019.
2. Simon Gibbons and Warunya Arunotayanun. *Novel Psychoactive Substances: Classification, Pharmacology and Toxicology*, Chapter 14: Natural Product (Fungal and Herbal) Novel Psychoactive Substances, 345–362. London: Academic Press, 2013.
3. Daniel Perkins et al. "Influence of Context and Setting on the Mental Health and Well-Being Outcomes of Ayahuasca Drinkers: Results of a Large International Survey." *Frontiers in Pharmacology* 12 (April 21, 2021): 623979.
4. https://www.hopkinsmedicine.org/news/newsroom/news-releases/johns-hopkins-launches-center-for-psychedelic-research

## CHAPTER 6. FROM RECOVERY TO REGENERATION

1. Richard Rohr. *Breathing under Water: Spirituality and the Twelve Steps*. Franciscan Media, 2021.
2. *Addictionary*. Recovery Research Institute. www.recoveryanswers.org/addiction-ary.
3. John W. James and Russell Friedman. *The Grief Recovery Handbook*. 20th Anniversary Expanded Edition. New York: Harper Perennial, 2014.
4. David Kessler. *Finding Meaning: The Sixth Stage of Grief*. New York: Simon and Schuster, 2019.

## CHAPTER 7. THE *OTHER* F WORD AND LIFE ON THE OTHER SIDE

1. Michael E. McCullough. "Forgiveness: Who Does It and How Do They Do It?" *Current Directions in Psychological Science* 10, no. 6 (2001).
2. Frederick A. DiBlasio. "Decision Based Forgiveness Treatment in Cases of Marital Infidelity." *Psychotherapy: Theory, Research, Practice, Training* 37, no. 2, Summer 2000: 149–158.

# Notes

3. LY Thompson, CR Snyder, L Hoffman, ST Michael, HN Rasmussen, LS Billings, L Heinze, JE Neufeld, HS Shorey, JC Roberts, DE Roberts. "Dispositional Forgiveness of Self, Others, and Situations." *Journal of Personality* 73, no. 2 (April 2005): 313–59. doi: 10.1111/j.1467-6494.2005.00311.x. PMID: 15745433

4. E. L. Worthington, Jr. (2020). Understanding Forgiveness of Other People: Definitions, Theories, and Processes, in *Handbook of Forgiveness, 2nd Ed.*, edited by E. L. Worthington, Jr., and N. G. Wade. New York: Routledge, pp. 11–21. doi:10.4324/9781351123341-2

5. Robert D. Enright, Suzanne Freedman, and Julio Rique. "The Psychology of Interpersonal Forgiveness," in *Exploring Forgiveness*, edited by Robert D. Enright and Joanna North. Madison, WI: University of Wisconsin Press, 1998, pp. 46–47.

INDEX

# Index

# Index

# Index

273

# Index

Stephanie Sarazin is a writer, researcher, and experiential expert in ambiguous grief. Her work began with her own experience of mid-life trauma, which sparked an ambitious journey—spiritually and around the world—to understand, name, and heal the grief she found within her. Her efforts revealed a first-of-its-kind definition for "ambiguous grief," whereby grief is onset by the loss of a loved one who is still living and wherein the experience of hope presents as a stage of the grieving process. Stephanie's work brings new resources to reframe disruptive, activating events as a gateway to discovering your highest self, in turn championing ambiguous grief as nuanced, natural, and navigable.

Stephanie is also the founder of RiseUpRooted, an online resource center for those navigating ambiguous grief, a grief educator, and a TEDx curator in her community.

She is an avid reader and a recreational runner, and lives in North Carolina, where she is currently training to hike to Mt. Everest's Base Camp.